Mastering the Medical Science Liaison Career Path

This book provides a comprehensive, practical guide to breaking into and excelling in Medical Science Liaison (MSL) roles—one of the pharmaceutical industry's most strategically important yet misunderstood positions. Through patient impact stories, actionable frameworks, and insider insights, this book transforms the daunting MSL job search into a strategic, relationship-driven process while preparing readers for long-term career success.

Key Features

- Unique Positioning: Treats MSL job search as relationship-building preparation for actual role success
- Practical Depth: Moves beyond generic advice to provide specific frameworks, templates, and industry insider knowledge
- Future Proofing: Integrates AI revolution in medical affairs—a topic absent from existing materials
- Authentic Voice: Written by a practicing MSL with demonstrated success across multiple therapeutic areas and organizations
- Patient-Impact Focus: Grounds career advice in meaningful healthcare outcomes rather than purely transactional objectives

Global Science Education

Professor Ali Eftekhari
Series Editor

Learning about the scientific education systems in the global context is of utmost importance now for two reasons. Firstly, the academic community is now international. It is no longer limited to top universities, as the mobility of staff and students is very common even in remote places. Secondly, education systems need to continually evolve in order to cope with the market demand. Contrary to the past when the pioneering countries were the most innovative ones, now emerging economies are more eager to push the boundaries of innovative education. Here, an overall picture of the whole field is provided. Moreover, the entire collection is indeed an encyclopaedia of science education and can be used as a resource for global education.

Series List:

Advancing Professional Development through CPE in Public Health
Ira Nurmala and Yashwant Pathak

A Spotlight on the History of Ancient Egyptian Medicine
Ibrahim M. Eltorai

Scientific Misconduct Training Workbook
John Gaetano D'Angelo

The Whats of a Scientific Life
John R. Helliwell

Inquiry-Based Science Education
Robyn M. Gillies

Hark, Hark! Hear the Story of a Science Educator
Jazlin Ebenezer

Miraculous Medicines and the Chemistry of Drug Design
Nathan Keighley

The Whens and Wheres of a Scientific Life
John R. Helliwell

www.routledge.com/Global-Science-Education/book-series/GSESERIES

Mastering the Medical Science Liaison Career Path

The Science of Influence

Evan Pasha

CRC Press
Taylor & Francis Group
Boca Raton London New York

CRC Press is an imprint of the
Taylor & Francis Group, an **informa** business

First edition published 2026
by CRC Press
2385 NW Executive Center Drive, Suite 320, Boca Raton FL 33431

and by CRC Press
4 Park Square, Milton Park, Abingdon, Oxon, OX14 4RN

CRC Press is an imprint of Taylor & Francis Group, LLC

ISBN: 9781041319665 (hbk)
ISBN: 9781041319672 (pbk)
ISBN: 9781003781547 (ebk)

DOI: 10.1201/9781003781547

Typeset in Times
by Newgen Publishing UK

Contents

Foreword

The Medical Science Liaison (MSL) role has undergone a profound transformation during my two decades in pharmaceutical medical affairs. What began as a primarily educational function has evolved into one of the most strategically important positions in our industry—requiring sophisticated understanding of clinical science, health economics, regulatory landscapes, and stakeholder engagement that extends far beyond traditional academic training.

Having started my career in pharma as an MSL, and having worked across multiple therapeutic areas and organizations, from large pharmaceutical companies to innovative biotech firms, I've witnessed firsthand how exceptional MSLs create ripple effects that extend far beyond individual stakeholder interactions. The most successful MSLs understand that their influence operates at the intersection of scientific rigor, authentic relationship building, and strategic thinking—a combination that can literally change the trajectory of patient care.

I've had the privilege of collaborating closely with the author of this book across two distinct but equally challenging therapeutic launches that exemplify the complexity and impact potential of modern medical affairs work. At Bristol Myers Squibb, we partnered on introducing the first cardiac myosin inhibitor for obstructive hypertrophic cardiomyopathy—a breakthrough therapy that required sophisticated stakeholder education about a complex disease mechanism and careful coordination across cardiology subspecialties to ensure optimal patient identification and care coordination. Later at AstraZeneca, we collaborated on the launch of an innovative antisense oligonucleotide in rare disease, where success demanded not just clinical expertise but deep understanding of patient advocacy groups, specialized care centers, and the unique challenges facing families affected by rare conditions.

Perhaps most significantly, we worked together to develop scientific narratives addressing health equity in transthyretin amyloidosis and to champion integration of health equity principles into field medical strategy. This collaboration highlighted one of the most critical evolutions in medical affairs: the recognition that scientific excellence must be coupled with deep understanding of healthcare disparities and commitment to ensuring that therapeutic advances reach all patients who can benefit, regardless of geographic location, socioeconomic status, or healthcare access barriers.

These experiences reinforced my conviction that the MSL role requires far more than clinical knowledge or scientific communication skills. Success demands strategic thinking that can navigate complex stakeholder ecosystems, authentic relationship building that creates lasting professional partnerships, and persistent commitment to removing barriers that prevent optimal patient care. The author demonstrated these competencies consistently, approaching each challenge with intellectual curiosity, collaborative spirit, and unwavering focus on patient impact.

What strikes me most about this book is its recognition that MSL success emerges from mastering both the art and science of influence. The scientific foundation—understanding clinical data, competitive landscapes, and regulatory implications—provides credibility and enables meaningful dialogue with healthcare stakeholders. But the art lies in building authentic relationships, identifying strategic opportunities, and creating collaborative solutions to complex healthcare challenges. This integration cannot be taught through traditional academic training; it emerges from putting yourself out there, understanding the context in which medical affairs operates, and developing the relationship management skills that enable sustained impact.

The book addresses three critical needs I consistently observe among medical affairs professionals. First, establishing the right mindset for MSL success requires moving beyond clinical or research paradigms to embrace the role of strategic territory CEO who orchestrates complex stakeholder ecosystems. This mental shift often represents the greatest challenge for healthcare professionals transitioning into industry roles, yet it's fundamental to creating the kind of strategic impact that defines exceptional MSL performance.

Second, the increasingly competitive landscape for MSL roles demands sophisticated job search strategies that go beyond traditional resume submissions. The networking approaches, interview preparation techniques, and personal branding strategies outlined in this book reflect the realities of a market where hundreds of qualified candidates may compete for a single position. Success requires transforming yourself from an anonymous applicant to a known quantity with internal advocates who can speak to your potential contributions.

Third, the integration of artificial intelligence into medical affairs workflows represents both unprecedented opportunity and competitive necessity. MSLs who master these technologies while maintaining the human expertise that defines their value proposition will create significant advantages in an increasingly sophisticated marketplace. The book's approach to AI adoption—emphasizing amplification of human capabilities rather than replacement—aligns perfectly with my own observations about how technology can enhance rather than threaten the strategic relationship building that defines exceptional medical affairs work.

The timing of this book could not be more appropriate. The pharmaceutical industry continues evolving rapidly, driven by scientific breakthroughs in gene therapy, cell therapy, and precision medicine that demand increasingly sophisticated medical affairs support. Regulatory environments grow more complex, requiring deeper understanding of real-world evidence generation and health economics. Stakeholder expectations continue elevating, with healthcare providers seeking strategic partners who can provide not just clinical education but practical solutions to implementation challenges.

Simultaneously, the talent pipeline for medical affairs roles faces significant pressure. The attractiveness of MSL careers has increased substantially, creating intense competition for opportunities while raising performance expectations. Organizations seek professionals who can contribute immediately while growing into broader strategic responsibilities over time. This dynamic makes resources like this book essential for both aspiring MSLs and experienced professionals seeking career advancement.

The book's practical orientation particularly resonates with my experience leading medical affairs teams. The frameworks for stakeholder mapping, the approaches to scientific communication, and the strategies for insight generation reflect real-world challenges that MSLs face daily. More importantly, the emphasis on authentic relationship building and value creation aligns with the sustainable approaches that create lasting impact rather than short-term tactical wins.

As I consider the future of medical affairs, I'm convinced that the principles outlined in this book will become even more relevant. The increasing complexity of therapeutic landscapes, the growing emphasis on personalized medicine, and the continued evolution of healthcare delivery models all demand MSLs who can think strategically, build authentic partnerships, and create collaborative solutions to complex challenges.

For aspiring MSLs, this book provides a comprehensive roadmap for breaking into a competitive field while developing the mindset and capabilities necessary for long-term success. For experienced professionals, it offers frameworks for elevating their strategic impact and advancing their careers in an evolving landscape. For organizations, it represents an investment in developing the kind of medical affairs capabilities that drive sustainable competitive advantage.

The author's commitment to excellence in medical affairs, demonstrated through our collaborations and his broader professional contributions, makes him uniquely qualified to guide others on this journey. His understanding of both the strategic imperatives and practical realities of MSL work, combined with his forward-looking perspective on technological integration, positions this book as an invaluable resource for anyone committed to creating meaningful impact through medical affairs excellence.

What defines exceptional MSL performance begins with understanding that your ultimate success is measured not by individual achievements, but by the collective impact you create through strategic relationship building, evidence-based education, and persistent commitment to advancing patient care. *Mastering the Medical Science Liaison Career Path* provides the blueprint for mastering that science while building a personally fulfilling career that contributes meaningfully to human health.

Leticia Ferri, MD
Vice President, Medical Affairs

Preface

THE HIDDEN HAND BEHIND PATIENT CARE

"The most profound impact often comes from work that remains invisible to those who benefit from it most.... I wrote this book to be the resource that I wish I had when I was breaking into industry transitioning from a postdoctoral scientist to an MSL."

Doctor's offices had always made John nervous, though he couldn't quite articulate why. Perhaps it was the difficulty accessing care in his rural community, the constant barrage of medical jargon that left him feeling confused, or the persistent sense that his healthcare providers weren't truly listening to his concerns. Whatever the reason, John consistently avoided seeking medical attention—a tendency that nearly cost him everything.

For months, John had been experiencing an unusual tingling sensation in his thumb, index, and ring fingers on both hands. The symptoms were particularly severe at night, often jolting him awake with a pins-and-needles sensation that required him to shake his hands vigorously for relief. At 58, John rationalized these episodes as simply part of getting older—after all, didn't everyone develop aches and pains with age?

The wake-up call came on a Tuesday evening while preparing dinner for his wife. As John reached for his favorite chef's knife to dice vegetables, his grip suddenly failed him completely. The eight-inch blade slipped from his fingers and plummeted toward the floor, the sharp point embedding itself in the hardwood mere inches from his feet. This near-miss forced John to confront what he'd been ignoring: something was seriously wrong.

A JOURNEY THROUGH THE HEALTHCARE SYSTEM

What followed was a healthcare journey that, in retrospect, seems almost miraculous in its coordination and precision. John's primary care physician quickly referred him to the right neurologist. The neurologist efficiently diagnosed his carpal tunnel syndrome and connected him with an expert orthopedic surgeon. During routine surgery, the surgeon had the foresight to send tissue samples for specialized testing that revealed amyloid deposits. This discovery led to genetic testing that confirmed hereditary transthyretin amyloidosis (hATTR)—a rare, progressive, and fatal disease.

But the story didn't end with diagnosis. John was seamlessly connected with a multidisciplinary team including a neuromuscular specialist who prescribed life-saving targeted therapy, a cardiologist who established crucial cardiac monitoring protocols, and a genetic counselor who guided his family through testing that revealed two of his three children carried the same genetic mutation and were at risk for developing the disease. Early detection allowed for preventive monitoring that could spare his children the devastating progression John might have faced.

Throughout this journey, John marveled at the coordination, expertise, and genuine care that guided him from mysterious symptoms to definitive diagnosis and optimal treatment. The right specialists seemed to appear at exactly the right moments. Each physician understood not just their own role, but how their work connected to a broader care strategy. Resources like free genetic testing and patient registries were readily available. Most remarkably, this entire complex care coordination unfolded smoothly and efficiently.

THE INVISIBLE INFLUENCE

What John never realized—and what most patients never understand—is that his exceptional care experience didn't happen by accident. Behind the scenes, a Medical Science Liaison (MSL) had spent months laying the groundwork that made John's coordinated care possible.

At no point did John directly interact with this MSL. He never knew this professional existed. Yet this individual's strategic work was instrumental in creating the conditions that led to John's timely diagnosis, optimal treatment, and ultimately, the preservation of his quality of life and potentially saved his life.

The MSL had recognized that carpal tunnel syndrome was often an early manifestation of hATTR, yet most orthopedic surgeons were unaware of this connection. Through persistent, scientifically focused outreach, the MSL educated John's future surgeon about when to suspect systemic amyloidosis and how to pursue further evaluation.

The MSL organized a multidisciplinary educational dinner that brought together the exact specialists who would later coordinate John's care—the orthopedic surgeon, neuromuscular neurologist, and cardiologist. These individuals were identified through meticulous profiling and identification of their specific interest in amyloidosis. This meeting established communication channels, care pathways, and collaborative relationships that proved crucial when John needed them months later.

The MSL also recommended the cardiologist to their pharmaceutical company as a principal investigator for a patient registry study—the same study John would eventually join, contributing to research that will benefit future patients with his condition.

UNDERSTANDING THE MSL ROLE

John's story illustrates the profound, often invisible impact that MSLs have on patient care. MSLs don't treat patients directly, yet their work creates the conditions that enable optimal patient outcomes. They operate at the intersection of science and strategy, building relationships, facilitating education, and connecting the right people at the right times to advance patient care.

This is what MSLs do: they work behind the scenes to ensure that scientific advances translate into clinical practice improvements. They identify gaps in medical knowledge and develop strategic approaches to address them. They build bridges between different medical specialties, creating collaborative networks that benefit patients with complex conditions. They connect clinicians with research opportunities that advance medical understanding.

Without the MSL's strategic efforts, John's story might have unfolded very differently. His carpal tunnel symptoms might have been treated in isolation, without recognition of the underlying systemic disease. His hATTR could have progressed to severe neuropathy, leaving him wheelchair-bound. Eventually, amyloid deposits might have infiltrated his heart, leading to heart failure and premature death. His children might never have learned about their genetic risk and ultimately shared the same fate as their father.

Instead, John received coordinated, expert care that halted his disease progression, preserved his function, and created a generational impact on his family's health. This transformation occurred because an MSL understood both the science of hATTR and the strategic importance of building the right relationships and educational frameworks to support optimal patient care.

WHY THIS BOOK MATTERS

As I reflect on John's journey and countless similar stories I've witnessed throughout my career in medical affairs, I'm struck by how few people—including many healthcare professionals—truly understand what MSLs do or why their work matters so profoundly.

I wrote this book to be the resource that I wish I had when I was breaking into industry transitioning from a postdoctoral scientist to an MSL. This book exists to decode the MSL role, not just for those considering this career path, but for anyone who wants to understand how scientific advances reach patients. The MSL profession represents one of the most dynamic, strategically important, and personally fulfilling career opportunities in healthcare today. Yet it remains widely misunderstood, even by many who might be perfectly suited for this work.

Whether you're a physician looking to expand your impact beyond individual patient encounters, a researcher seeking to bridge the gap between discovery and application, or a pharmacist wanting to contribute more directly to patient outcomes, the MSL role offers unique opportunities to create meaningful change in healthcare.

But success in medical affairs requires more than clinical knowledge or scientific expertise. It demands strategic thinking, relationship-building skills, business acumen, and the ability to work effectively across multiple disciplines and organizations. It requires understanding not just the science, but how that science fits into the broader healthcare ecosystem.

This book will take you behind the scenes of medical affairs work, showing you exactly how MSLs create impact like John's story represents. You'll learn how to build the knowledge, skills, and relationships necessary to excel in this field. Most importantly, you'll discover how to find your own "why"—your personal motivation for pursuing work that can literally save lives through strategic scientific influence.

Before continuing your journey through these pages, I encourage you to reflect on your own motivation. What draws you to the intersection of science and patient care? How might you contribute to ensuring that scientific advances reach the patients who need them most? What kind of impact do you want to create in healthcare?

The answers to these questions will guide you not just through this book, but through a career that offers the unique satisfaction of knowing that your work—though often invisible to the patients who benefit from it—creates ripple effects that extend far beyond any single interaction or relationship.

John's story is one of countless examples of how MSLs work behind the scenes to positively impact patients. Not every day in medical affairs leads to outcomes this dramatic, but the potential for meaningful impact exists in every scientific discussion, every educational program, and every relationship you build as an MSL.

This is the hidden hand that guides much of modern healthcare's most important advances from bench to bedside. This is the work of MSLs.

This is why it matters.

Welcome to Mastering the Medical Science Liaison Career Path. Let's begin your journey toward a career that can change not just your professional trajectory, but the lives of patients you may never meet.

About the Author

Evan Pasha, PhD, is an award-winning Medical Science Liaison with clinical research and medical affairs experiences spanning cardiovascular disease, neurology, immunology, and rare diseases. He earned his PhD in Kinesiology from The University of Texas at Austin. Following his doctoral work, Dr. Pasha completed a Postdoctoral Research Fellowship at the Institute of Exercise and Environmental Medicine at UT Southwestern Medical Center, where he continued his scholarly work. With over 30 peer reviewed publications, his research focuses on the intersection of cardiovascular health, neuroplasticity, and aging. Currently serving as a Senior Medical Science Liaison, Dr. Pasha has held progressive roles in medical affairs where he has lived the journey outlined in the book.

The MSL as Territory CEO

1

Mastering Stakeholder Collaboration and Strategic Influence

"The most successful MSLs understand that they are not just scientific liaisons—they are the CEOs of complex ecosystems where every relationship matters and every collaboration can impact patient care."

When describing a day in the life of a Medical Science Liaison (MSL), very few are truly the same. The MSL serves as the Swiss Army knife of medical affairs teams, wearing different hats on different days, and sometimes more than one at a time. When aspiring MSLs ask about a "typical" day, only a surface-level answer can be communicated in a brief conversation. In reality, MSLs have an incredible breadth of roles and responsibilities that must be navigated within a complex interpersonal ecosystem.

A typical day might begin with scheduling 38 personalized introductory emails to send, followed by reviewing clinical trial data for an investigator meeting, pivot to collaborating with commercial colleagues on a complex access issue, continue with a virtual advisory board planning session, and end with drafting medical information responses for multiple clinical scenarios. The adaptability and strategic thinking required differs significantly from more structured task-oriented workplace environments.

Before diving into the specific tasks of what an MSL does, we must first understand the mindset of a successful MSL. The MSL is often described as

DOI: 10.1201/9781003781547-1

the "CEO" of their territory—a concept that proves critical for success. Once you land the role, you step into an intricate ecosystem of stakeholders. It becomes your responsibility as the CEO to procure deep knowledge about your territory, identify opportunities for development, uncover barriers to care, and implement actionable solutions all while being a trusted scientific colleague to your external stakeholders, the key opinion leaders (KOLs). After a careful assessment of what exists, you must determine what's needed, and do your best to make it happen.

THE CEO MINDSET AND CUSTOMER-CENTRIC APPROACH

To operate effectively as a territory CEO, you must first determine who your customers are and take the time to understand them thoroughly. In short, everyone is a customer. Although your coworkers function as teammates working toward a unified direction to improve patient care, they are also customers in the sense that they have their own specific objectives they are trying to accomplish. Conceptualizing internal stakeholders and colleagues as customers ensures that you don't take anyone for granted, always communicate cordially, and maintain your willingness to find collaborative opportunities.

This mindset shift is often one of the most challenging aspects of transitioning into an MSL role, particularly for healthcare professionals accustomed to more structured clinical environments. The transition requires learning to proactively shape priorities and create value for multiple stakeholders simultaneously, which demands a reevaluation of how to approach professional relationships and strategic planning.

Exceptional interpersonal skills represent the cornerstone of MSL success, as virtually every aspect of the role depends on effective collaboration. The ability to build trust, be engaging, facilitate productive relationships, and work seamlessly across diverse stakeholder groups is not merely advantageous—it is essential. MSLs who struggle with interpersonal dynamics will find themselves unable to achieve their strategic objectives, regardless of their scientific expertise. This collaborative imperative permeates every dimension of the role, from fostering productive team dynamics with fellow MSLs to cultivating strategic partnerships with external thought leaders and commercial colleagues.

INTERNAL STAKEHOLDER MAPPING

MSL Team Dynamics

Field medical MSL teams are carefully curated by regional field medical managers to be composed of different backgrounds (PhD, PharmD, APP, MD) that bring different skill sets and personalities to the table. This diversity creates tremendous opportunities for peer learning and collaborative problem-solving, but it also requires sophisticated team dynamics and mutual respect.

PhDs are often exceptional at understanding and teaching science but may need to develop stronger interpersonal soft skills, clinical knowledge, and understanding of the healthcare system. Pharmacists typically excel at understanding the product—its pharmacokinetic/pharmacodynamic profile, mechanism of action, and drug interactions—but may lack depth of understanding of the disease state and clinical practice patterns. Clinicians bring unparalleled clinical experience and are attuned to identifying barriers to care and potential solutions but may need to develop stronger research interpretation skills and learn to communicate scientific information in non-clinical contexts. Advanced practice providers combine clinical experience with practical healthcare delivery knowledge, often understanding both clinical care and healthcare economics.

As a collective, these differing perspectives, experiences, and expertise are relied upon to deliver the field medical strategy effectively. As an individual, you should feel confident in what you bring to the table but remain eager to learn from your colleagues. The most tenured MSL can learn from a newly minted MSL's fresh perspective just as the new MSL can learn from the tenured MSL's wisdom and experience.

There are endless opportunities for collaboration with other MSLs on myriad activities: conference planning and execution, journal clubs and scientific education sessions, field training and professional development programs, medical information creation and validation, territory cross-coverage during absences, insights sharing and synthesis, and competitive intelligence gathering. There may also be opportunities to collaborate with MSLs who support therapeutic areas outside of your own, such as facilitating introductions to KOLs, completing joint medically led programs, organizing cross-therapeutic roundtables, and aligning conference strategies.

Headquarters Medical Affairs Collaboration

Strong relationships with headquarters-based medical directors, evidence generation teams, and global medical team members represent important internal stakeholders who should also be viewed as customers. Their perspectives on important information that you are responsible to pull through to external KOLs shape medical narrative. You will also provide insights and feedback on that narrative based on your external interactions that may result in material changes to strategy. Through these collaborations, you will mutually benefit to accomplish strategic objectives that extend far beyond your individual external engagement with KOLs.

This reciprocal relationship enables MSLs to provide field-based insights that inform clinical development strategies, competitive positioning, and market access planning. Collaboration with evidence generation teams creates opportunities to translate field observations into formal research initiatives, support real-world evidence studies, and contribute to publication planning based on stakeholder relationships and market knowledge. MSLs also contribute valuable input to regulatory strategy, helping to ensure that field insights support regulatory submissions, labeling discussions, and post-market surveillance activities.

Understanding the strategic priorities and competitive challenges of marketing colleagues enables MSLs to provide medical insights that help them succeed while staying true to scientific mission. This shift in perspective transforms working relationships and creates much more strategic value for all parties involved.

COMMERCIAL TEAM COLLABORATION

Outside of the medical organization, you have a team within the commercial organization that can provide great value to your function. You must know your commercial counterparts, from your local salesperson and regional sales director to the thought leader liaison (TLL), access and reimbursement professionals, and anyone higher up in the commercial organization with whom you're able to generate a relationship. Take the time to get to know them on a personal level. At the very least, know who they are and where they sit in the organization. This will be easier at smaller companies compared with large more complex organizations.

Sales Team Partnership

Your local salesperson possesses distinct knowledge of the territory that complements your medical expertise. They know who the key external customers are from a commercial standpoint and can facilitate compliant introductions, provide contacts for hard-to-access office gatekeepers, help you navigate local politics between competing institutions, identify regional unmet clinical needs, uncover practice-specific barriers to care, and support basic logistics like knowing what day of the week a provider will be at a given location.

Open communication between MSLs and sales representatives enables healthcare provider offices to see your company as working in a coordinated way while being respectful of their time and efforts to deliver strong patient care. You are also a critical resource for the local salesperson because of your ability to reactively answer questions that are off-label, discuss clinical development activities and research, and address clinical concerns in ways they cannot due to regulatory constraints.

In the best-case scenario, there exists a symbiotic relationship where the MSL and salesperson work toward the common goal of supporting healthcare providers on behalf of patients. This requires clear understanding of respective roles, mutual respect for different objectives, and sophisticated coordination strategies that maximize value for healthcare providers while maintaining regulatory compliance.

The regional sales director represents another valuable ally who can support your objectives within the medical strategy. Together, you can align on regional conference activities, compliantly convey medical objectives to the commercial team, and identify areas within your geography where there may be an outsized need for medical support. A common complaint from the commercial organization is a lack of knowledge about the MSL's activities. Compliant communication of medical strategy, facilitated by the regional sales director, can build trust through transparency, and create opportunities for strategic coordination.

Thought Leader Liaison Collaboration

Another form of collaboration involves working with TLLs who form deep relationships with the upper echelon of KOLs. TLLs are a critical component of the commercial and marketing organization through their curation of the speaker's bureau—a group of physicians who are paid by the pharmaceutical company to speak about either a product or disease state.

As you're getting to know your region as its CEO, you'll uncover KOLs who either explicitly want to be on the speaker's bureau or wield strong regional influence but may not currently be speakers. You can recommend these KOLs to the TLL and commercial organization as candidates. This action brings value to both the KOL and your company by creating new opportunities for education and thought leadership while expanding your organization's network of expert advocates.

Access and Reimbursement Support

Barriers to care are rampant in clinical practice, but perhaps the most frustrating for health care providers (HCPs) are those related to access and reimbursement. As mentioned earlier, one of your many jobs as an MSL is to uncover these barriers and identify actionable solutions. In these cases, the answer is often simple: phone a friend. Although you will be trained on the basics of access and reimbursement for your therapy, there is often a specific role within your organization that can support healthcare providers with the detailed specifics.

It's your job to uncover the barrier and connect the right person to address the HCP's need. Holding a strong relationship with this internal customer may enable a patient to access a life-changing therapy and can significantly impact treatment outcomes. Understanding the access and reimbursement landscape also helps you provide more complete support to healthcare providers who are trying to navigate complex insurance requirements and prior authorization processes.

EXTERNAL STAKEHOLDER RELATIONSHIPS

Now that we better understand the internal customer environment, let's examine external stakeholders (see Figure 1.1). KOLs come in many shapes and sizes, each providing different tiers of value to your organization and requiring different engagement strategies.

Understanding KOL Tiers and Influence

In the most basic sense, a KOL is someone who has a significant sphere of influence over other healthcare providers or scientists. These individuals have the

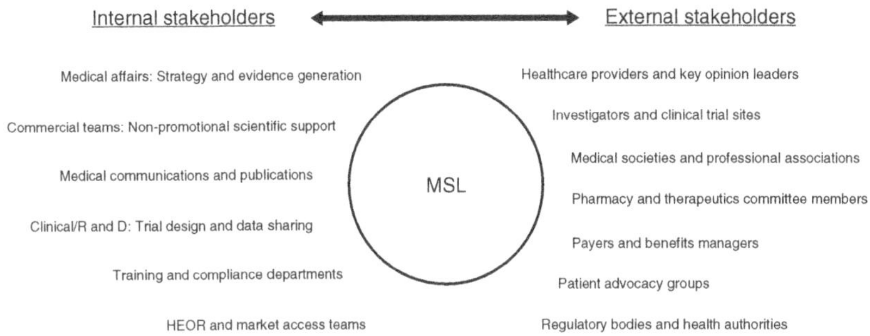

FIGURE 1.1 The MSL as Central Hub in a Complex Stakeholder Ecosystem.

power to affect treatment paradigms, influence peer behavior, drive adoption of new therapies, and guide evidence generation. They exist at the international, national, regional, or local levels, each requiring different approaches and offering different strategic value.

International/Global KOLs represent the highest tier of influence, with recognition and impact that extends across multiple countries and healthcare systems. These individuals typically hold prestigious academic positions, lead international research consortiums, serve on global medical society leadership teams, and influence worldwide treatment guidelines. They frequently speak at major international conferences, author high-impact publications, and collaborate on multinational research initiatives. Examples include department chairs at top-tier academic medical centers who lead international clinical trials, presidents of global medical societies, or physicians who chair international treatment guideline committees.

National KOLs wield significant influence within their home countries, often serving as the bridge between global medical developments and national healthcare policy and practice. They typically hold leadership positions in national medical societies, serve on national treatment guideline committees, and are frequently invited to speak at major national conferences. They may chair departments at prestigious academic medical centers, lead national research initiatives, or serve as principal investigators for landmark clinical trials. Their influence extends across multiple regions within their country and they often mentor the next generation of medical leaders.

Regional KOLs possess strong influence within specific geographic regions or large healthcare systems. This may include department heads at major regional medical centers who organize regional meetings, serve as presidents of regional chapters for national organizations, or lead multi-institutional research collaborations. They often serve as the connection point between national medical developments and local clinical practice, helping to translate broader treatment recommendations into regional implementation strategies. Regional KOLs frequently mentor local physicians and may serve on regional hospital committees or healthcare system leadership teams.

Local KOLs represent the foundation of clinical influence, delivering care outside of large academic centers while wielding significant geographic or institutional influence. These may include community practice leaders who are respected by their peers, chief medical officers at community hospitals, or department heads at local medical centers. Chief residents, fellows, or clinical pharmacists who support training of healthcare providers may also serve as strong influencers within a health system for driving education and practice change. Local KOLs are often the most directly connected to day-to-day patient care and can provide valuable insights about real-world treatment challenges and implementation barriers.

Emerging and Digital KOLs represent growing categories of influence that transcend traditional geographic and institutional boundaries. These individuals may be younger physicians who leverage digital platforms and social media for professional communication, researchers who are gaining recognition through innovative work or novel approaches, or healthcare providers who have developed significant online followings through medical education content. Digital KOLs are particularly important for reaching younger healthcare providers and understanding how medical information spreads through modern communication channels.

STRATEGIC TERRITORY MANAGEMENT

Your role as the MSL is to identify these individuals across all tiers and allocate your time and resources accordingly to implement your company's medical strategy effectively. Your list of KOL customers is living and should be constantly scrutinized and updated. Younger healthcare providers advance in their careers and become top-tier KOLs, and these developing relationships become increasingly valuable over time. Conversely, top-tier KOLs may eventually take a step back in favor of greater emphasis on their family life, and their influence may recede, requiring you to adjust your engagement strategy accordingly. Career trajectories are not always linear and your ability to recognize and adapt to these changes is a major strength.

As the CEO of your territory, you must know all the players on the field and understand how they are interconnected. This requires sophisticated mapping of professional networks, institutional relationships, and influence patterns that shape how medical decisions are made in your region. Organizations will sometimes have tools such as VeevaLink or Komodo to assist you in mapping your territory and identifying the key players. Ultimately you need to understand not just who the influential people are, but how they relate to each other, where they source their information, and what motivates their professional decisions.

After completing this essential fact-finding and relationship mapping, you can begin to wield your own influence strategically and have the profound impact on patient care that likely motivated your career transition into medical affairs. This influence is exercised not through direct patient care, but through educating and supporting the healthcare providers who treat thousands of patients, amplifying your impact exponentially.

THE ORCHESTRATED ECOSYSTEM

The complexity of the MSL role ultimately stems from its position at the center of multiple intersecting ecosystems. Success requires mastering the art of stakeholder collaboration while maintaining scientific integrity, strategic focus, and genuine commitment to improving patient outcomes. The most effective MSLs develop sophisticated understanding of how these various relationships and collaborations create value that extends far beyond any individual interaction.

Every relationship you build, every collaboration you foster, and every barrier you help overcome creates ripple effects throughout your territory's healthcare ecosystem. When you help a sales representative understand complex clinical data, you enable them to have more meaningful conversations with healthcare providers. When you collaborate with colleagues to develop educational content, you leverage complementary expertise to create resources that may influence clinical practice. When you connect a healthcare provider with the right access specialist, you may enable a patient to receive life-changing therapy.

The territory CEO mindset recognizes that these seemingly disparate activities are actually interconnected elements of a comprehensive strategy to improve patient care through strategic relationship building, collaborative problem-solving, and evidence-based influence. Your success as an MSL depends not on any single skill or relationship, but on your ability to orchestrate this complex ecosystem effectively.

As you develop in your MSL role, you will become the ultimate "Swiss Army knife" who is more than just versatile. You will have the capability to integrate your specialized skills into a cohesive workflow that can address diverse challenges effectively. Your ability to seamlessly transition between scientific educator, strategic collaborator, relationship builder, and barrier-buster will determine your ultimate impact on the patients whose lives you touch through the healthcare providers you support.

The day-to-day variety that initially seems overwhelming becomes the source of intellectual stimulation and professional satisfaction that makes the MSL role uniquely rewarding. Every day presents new opportunities to create value, solve problems, and contribute to the advancement of medical knowledge and patient care. In this dynamic environment, the only constant is change—and the most successful MSLs learn to thrive in this complexity while never losing sight of their ultimate mission: improving patient outcomes through strategic scientific influence.

Understanding your territory as a complex ecosystem of interconnected stakeholders, viewing all collaborators as customers with specific needs, and developing sophisticated strategies for relationship building and value creation will position you for success as the CEO of your territory. The amplified impact you can achieve through strategic collaboration and influence makes the MSL role one of the most rewarding paths for healthcare professionals who want to impact patient care at scale.

CHAPTER 1 TAKEAWAYS: TERRITORY CEO MASTERY

Mindset Development

- Do you understand the CEO mindset and how it applies to territory management?
- Can you identify all stakeholders in your ecosystem as customers with specific needs?
- Have you developed strategies for proactive opportunity identification?

Collaboration Mastery

- Can you leverage complementary expertise within your MSL team effectively?
- Do you understand how to create value for commercial colleagues while maintaining scientific integrity?
- Have you developed strong relationships with headquarters medical affairs teams?

Stakeholder Management

- Can you identify and categorize KOLs across all influence tiers?
- Do you understand the interconnections between different stakeholders in your territory?
- Have you developed systematic approaches to relationship building and maintenance?

Strategic Integration

- Can you see how individual collaborations contribute to broader strategic objectives?
- Do you understand how to amplify your impact through effective relationship orchestration?
- Have you developed approaches to continuous learning and adaptation in your territory?

Core MSL Responsibilities 2

The Foundation of Scientific Impact

"Success as an MSL comes from seamlessly weaving together scientific expertise, authentic relationships, strategic thinking, and relentless curiosity into a unified approach that serves both healthcare providers and patients."

Now that we understand where the Medical Science Liaison (MSL) sits within the context of internal and external stakeholder ecosystems, we can explore the diverse and interconnected responsibilities that define this multifaceted position. The MSL role encompasses several fundamental components that work synergistically to create strategic value: conducting scientific exchange with healthcare providers and key opinion leaders to address complex clinical questions; building enduring professional relationships based on trust and mutual value creation; maintaining active presence at medical conferences and scientific congresses; and systematically gathering actionable insights that inform organizational strategy and decision-making.

Success in the MSL role requires the ability to seamlessly integrate these diverse responsibilities while maintaining scientific integrity, regulatory compliance, and a steadfast commitment to advancing medical knowledge in service of patient care. The complexity and strategic importance of these combined functions position MSLs as critical assets within pharmaceutical organizations, serving as the essential bridge between cutting-edge research and real-world clinical practice.

Each responsibility builds upon and reinforces the others, creating a comprehensive approach to scientific influence that extends far beyond any single interaction or activity. Understanding how these components interconnect and amplify each other is crucial for MSL success and strategic impact.

DOI: 10.1201/9781003781547-2

SCIENTIFIC EXCHANGE: THE ART OF VALUE-DRIVEN COMMUNICATION

The cornerstone of MSL effectiveness lies in the ability to conduct meaningful scientific exchange that creates genuine value for healthcare stakeholders. With any external engagement, the overarching goal must be value creation, as KOLs are stepping away from critically important tasks—patient care, documentation, peer-to-peer consultations, grant writing, research endeavors, or personal time with family—to engage with you. Their time represents an extraordinarily valuable resource, and you must be prepared to provide commensurate value in return.

Defining Scientific Exchange in Practice

Scientific exchange, in its essence, represents bidirectional, evidence-based communication of medical and scientific information between MSLs and healthcare stakeholders. The primary purpose extends beyond simple information sharing. The goal is to advance clinical knowledge, improve patient care, and address unmet medical needs through collaborative dialogue. The MSL's role maintains an inherently non-promotional nature, and scientific exchange must consistently reflect this boundary while providing substantial educational value.

Success in scientific exchange occurs when the KOL views you as a valued extension of their own educational ambitions to stay current in clinical practice and scientific advancement. This perception transforms the MSL from an external vendor into a trusted scientific partner who contributes meaningfully to the healthcare provider's professional development and clinical effectiveness.

Strategic Context and Narrative Development

Scientific exchange occurs within the context of your pharmaceutical company's broader scientific narrative, but this context must never override the educational focus or appear promotional. During interactions, this might involve sharing recent publications that could shift a clinician's perspective about a disease state, presenting new research that reveals previously unrecognized clinical patterns, or discussing emerging treatment paradigms that address unmet medical needs.

For example, you might share a recent publication demonstrating that symptomatology in a specific patient population is more severe or common than previously believed. This represents important disease state education that identifies a significant unmet medical need for the healthcare provider. If the therapy you represent has evidence of efficacy for those specific symptoms, the disease state education you provided creates a natural educational opportunity to discuss the clinical trial data that led to your therapeutic's approval.

The KOL may not have been aware that your company's product is a therapeutic option for the patient population you described, creating an opportunity to educate about the safety and efficacy profile of the treatment. However, this transition must occur naturally within the scientific dialogue and maintain educational focus rather than promotional intent.

Fair and Balanced Communication Standards

Of critical importance, any time clinical data is shared, it must be presented in a fair and balanced manner that reflects scientific integrity and regulatory requirements. Whenever you discuss efficacy data, you must also address safety considerations with equal transparency and detail. This fair and balanced approach is mandated for regulatory compliance, but it also serves the equally important purpose of maintaining your reputation as a truthful, reliable scientific resource.

Emphasizing efficacy while minimizing safety concerns undermines your credibility as a non-promotional scientific partner and can permanently damage the trust that forms the foundation of effective MSL relationships. Healthcare providers depend on receiving complete, objective information to make informed clinical decisions, and any perception that information is being selectively presented will tarnish the collaborative relationship that enables effective scientific exchange.

Preparation and Customization Strategies

When selecting materials for scientific exchange—whether disease state information or product-related data—thorough preparation becomes essential for creating value and maintaining credibility. This preparation involves two critical components that must be executed meticulously.

First, develop comprehensive understanding of your KOL, including their specific clinical and research interests, baseline knowledge level, patient populations, institutional priorities, and communication preferences. The most prominent KOLs may already possess more detailed knowledge about the data you planned to present than you do. Understanding their expertise level and interests enables you to tailor your approach appropriately and avoid the cardinal sin of presenting elementary information to sophisticated experts.

Second, master the content you plan to present with sufficient depth to handle detailed questions and adapt your presentation level as needed. Anticipate potential questions and prepare to shift seamlessly from high-level overviews to granular detail based on the healthcare provider's interests and expertise. The same information presentation will not be appropriate for every KOL, so developing the ability to customize scientific exchange to meet specific stakeholder needs becomes crucial for providing genuine value.

However, even the best-laid plans can go sideways quickly. You may walk into an office full of confidence with your well-rehearsed presentation on a new publication, only to have the KOL stop you ten seconds in to ask about a completely separate topic. This can happen in your first meeting or your tenth meeting, and you must always be ready to adapt and go with the flow. If it's a question or new topic you can address, dive right in. If it's not, don't panic. This situation presents an opportunity to ask open-ended questions, gain insights, understand what they truly value, and secure future time to return with that specific information. Then, ideally, you can steer back to your planned topic or weave it into the conversation if it's related. Regardless of your preparedness for this new topic, remain calm and curious to navigate effectively—your ability to adapt while maintaining credibility often matters more than delivering your prepared material perfectly.

Advanced Scientific Exchange Techniques

Experienced MSLs develop sophisticated approaches to scientific exchange that go beyond simple information delivery. These include facilitating collaborative analysis of clinical scenarios, encouraging critical evaluation of research methodologies, exploring practical implementation challenges for new evidence, and connecting disparate research findings to create broader understanding of therapeutic landscapes.

The most effective scientific exchanges become collaborative explorations where both the MSL and healthcare provider contribute insights, ask probing questions, and work together to understand the implications of new research for clinical practice. This collaborative approach transforms scientific exchange from a one-way information transfer into a dynamic professional dialogue that benefits both parties and creates lasting professional relationships.

BUILDING STRONG RELATIONSHIPS: THE FOUNDATION OF LONG-TERM IMPACT

The ability to secure a KOL's time and attention becomes significantly easier when they genuinely like and trust you as a professional colleague. While building initial rapport with a KOL can happen relatively quickly, developing the strong, enduring relationships that enable strategic collaboration requires sustained effort, consistency, and authentic value creation over time.

First Impressions and Communication Style Adaptation

First impressions carry disproportionate weight in professional relationship building, particularly in the time-constrained environment where most MSL–KOL interactions occur. From your initial conversation, including your email correspondence, pay careful attention to understanding how each KOL prefers to communicate. Some healthcare providers include extensive pleasantries and personal context in their communications, while others prefer brief, direct exchanges focused exclusively on scientific content.

Mirroring the communication style and professional tone that your KOL prefers demonstrates respect for their preferences and helps establish the initial foundation for productive collaboration. This adaptation should feel natural rather than forced and requires genuine attention to their communication patterns and preferences.

Value Proposition Development and Goal Alignment

In your introductory interactions, explicitly communicate the value you can provide while actively evaluating their professional goals and interests. Understanding what each KOL hopes to achieve through collaboration enables you to align your offerings with their objectives, creating genuine mutual benefit rather than one-sided requests for their time and expertise.

Some healthcare providers seek opportunities to join speaker bureaus, contribute to advisory boards, or participate in research initiatives. If they express interest in research partnerships, explore what types of research align with their interests and capabilities—clinical trials, patient registries, real-world evidence studies, investigator-sponsored research, or translational research. Understanding their research infrastructure, patient populations, and institutional support enables you to identify appropriate collaboration opportunities.

Other clinicians prioritize education, either for themselves or for colleagues within their healthcare system or broader professional community. Some healthcare providers manage extremely high patient volumes and struggle to stay current with rapidly evolving literature, making your role in scientific exchange particularly valuable for their professional development.

Caring genuinely about their objectives and finding ways to support their professional goals creates the foundation for continued engagement and collaboration. When you compliantly partner with KOLs to advance their legitimate professional objectives, you increase your value proposition while improving access to these important stakeholders for future initiatives from internal stakeholders across your organization.

Personal Connection and Authentic Relationship Building

While professional relationship building necessarily contains transactional elements, remember that KOLs are also humans with interests and passions extending beyond medicine and research. They enjoy traveling to new destinations, spending time at vacation homes, following sports teams, attending theater performances, or pursuing unique hobbies—one pharmacist I worked with enjoyed rebuilding vintage soda machines as a weekend hobby.

Explore these personal interests in appropriate, professional ways while sharing relevant aspects of your own background and interests. Perhaps you both attended the same graduate school and follow their athletic programs. Maybe they recently traveled to New York City for Broadway shows, or you're both navigating the challenges of parenting young children. These authentic personal connections can strengthen professional relationships and make your interactions more memorable and meaningful.

I once received invaluable potty-training advice for my toddler from a chief of cardiology during a round table dinner—a conversation that had nothing to do with medical affairs but everything to do with building a genuine human connection that enhanced our professional collaboration.

Authenticity and Consistency

Perhaps the most critical component of relationship building involves being consistently authentic across all interactions. Attempting to present different versions of yourself to different stakeholders is unsustainable and ultimately counterproductive. Being genuinely yourself across multiple interactions builds over time to solidify the KOL's perception of who you are, associates you with the specific value you provide, and establishes your reliability as a trusted professional partner.

This authenticity must extend to acknowledging the limitations of your knowledge, admitting when you don't know answers to questions, and following through consistently on commitments you make. Healthcare providers can quickly identify and lose respect for professionals who overstate their expertise or fail to deliver on promises.

Strong relationships built through this approach pay significant dividends during conferences, create opportunities for strategic collaboration, and contribute meaningfully to career advancement as your reputation for integrity and value creation spreads throughout the professional community and internally at your organization.

CONFERENCE PRESENCE: MAXIMIZING HIGH-VALUE INTERACTION OPPORTUNITIES

Medical conferences and scientific congresses represent concentrated opportunities for MSLs to demonstrate value, advance relationships, gather intelligence, and accelerate career development. Whether reconnecting with team members, meeting former colleagues, covering scientific sessions, or engaging with the most prominent experts in your field, conferences offer unparalleled opportunities for strategic relationship building and professional growth.

Strategic Conference Planning and Preparation

The work that enables successful conference outcomes begins months before the actual event. Your primary objective should be identifying which healthcare providers from your territory plan to attend, understanding their specific interests and session priorities, and developing a comprehensive engagement strategy that maximizes the value of these focused interaction opportunities.

National and regional conferences provide unique access to KOLs who are typically managing the constant demands of busy clinical practices, research responsibilities, and personal commitments. During conferences, these same individuals often have more flexibility in their schedules and greater openness to meaningful professional conversations without the time pressures they face at their typical work environment.

Beyond individual meetings, conferences create opportunities to organize roundtable discussions that bring KOLs from the same institution or therapeutic area together for collaborative dialogue about current treatment landscapes, emerging research directions, or clinical practice challenges. These group interactions can address medical information dissemination objectives while advancing specific initiatives your company emphasizes, such as diagnostic support tools or clinical decision support resources.

Scientific Session Coverage and Intelligence Gathering

Session coverage is a critical component of conference productivity that requires prioritization and systematic execution. Developing a clear understanding of which scientific content relates directly to your company's therapeutic areas while identifying sessions that specifically interest the KOLs you serve enables you to provide maximum value during subsequent interactions.

When you appear at your next meeting with detailed insights from specific sessions that the KOL missed, you demonstrate concrete value while reinforcing your position as a valuable scientific resource. This approach requires diligent session attendance, active engagement with presented content, and meticulous note-taking focused on gathering insights with both medical and commercial implications.

Some difficult-to-access KOLs may present research outside your primary therapeutic area or appear at sessions that wouldn't typically appear on your coverage list. Review conference mobile applications and printed schedules in advance to identify these opportunities, enabling you to introduce yourself immediately following their presentations when they can associate your name and face with introductory emails they may have previously overlooked.

Team Coordination and Booth Management

At larger conferences, MSL teams often share responsibility for staffing medical information booths, which requires careful coordination to balance this commitment with individual meeting schedules and session coverage priorities. Booth duty and scientific session coverage represent shared team responsibilities that must be carefully balanced against planned KOL meetings.

Developing comprehensive conference schedules that display all commitments in a single view clarifies potential conflicts and enables execution of successful conference strategies. This coordination becomes particularly important when managing simultaneous commitments to booth coverage, high-priority scientific sessions, and strategic stakeholder meetings.

Career Development and Professional Networking

Conferences also provide invaluable opportunities for career advancement and professional development. Remember that at the end of the day, *you* are your own most important stakeholder, and conferences bring together colleagues from across your broader medical organization who may not otherwise be accessible for career development conversations.

Schedule time with professionals from other medical affairs functions where you might want to grow your career. Engage with colleagues in evidence generation, medical training, launch excellence, medical affairs leadership, or executive roles. Introduce yourself to senior executives, arrange focused conversations with your direct manager, or connect with executive MSLs who can provide career guidance.

Use these in-person opportunities to gain knowledge about experiences you'll need to advance to your next role and beyond. Understand the competencies, relationships, and accomplishments that enable career progression while building the professional network that can support your long-term career objectives. Remember your CEO mindset and that everyone is a customer.

Finally, invest time in strengthening relationships with immediate teammates through appropriate social activities before returning to the isolation of territorial work. These team relationships provide professional support, collaborative opportunities, and personal connections that enhance job satisfaction and career resilience.

GATHERING MEDICAL INSIGHTS: TRANSFORMING INFORMATION INTO STRATEGIC INTELLIGENCE

Throughout all the aforementioned external activities—scientific exchange, relationship building, and conference participation—MSLs uncover invaluable intelligence in the form of actionable medical insights. These insights represent far more than simple data collection; they provide contextual understanding of how medical decisions are made, what barriers exist in clinical practice, and where opportunities exist to improve patient outcomes through strategic intervention.

Defining Medical Insights and Their Strategic Value

Medical insights are actionable intelligence derived from MSL interactions that reveal patterns, trends, care barriers, unmet medical needs, competitive dynamics, and strategic opportunities relevant to therapeutic areas, treatment approaches, and pharmaceutical business strategy. Unlike traditional market research data, medical insights emerge from ongoing scientific relationships and authentic clinical discussions, providing nuanced understanding of the complex factors that influence treatment decisions, adoption patterns, and clinical outcomes in real-world healthcare settings.

The most impactful MSLs consistently generate organization-changing insights that influence scientific narratives, inform clinical development, medical strategies, and business decisions. These high-value insights result from strong stakeholder relationships that enable candid conversations, combined with MSL expertise in identifying the right questions to ask and persistence in exploring important topics thoroughly.

Categories of Actionable Medical Intelligence

Clinical Practice Patterns and Real-World Usage: MSLs gather detailed insights about how healthcare providers use treatments in clinical practice, including patient selection criteria that may differ from clinical trial populations, dosing strategies adapted for real-world conditions, combination therapy approaches, and treatment sequencing decisions. This real-world usage data often differs significantly from clinical trial protocols and provides valuable intelligence for optimal therapeutic positioning, educational program development, and clinical research planning.

Unmet Medical Needs and Treatment Gaps: Through ongoing dialogue with practicing clinicians, MSLs identify specific gaps in current treatment options, patient populations with inadequate therapeutic choices, and clinical scenarios where new research or drug development could address significant healthcare challenges. These insights directly inform research and development priorities, clinical development strategies, and innovation pipeline decisions.

Competitive Intelligence and Market Dynamics: MSLs observe how competing products perform in real-world clinical settings, including comparative efficacy outcomes, safety profiles in diverse patient populations, access challenges, and healthcare provider satisfaction levels. This competitive intelligence enables companies to understand their market position accurately, identify opportunities for differentiation, and develop responsive strategic positioning.

Treatment Barriers and Access Challenges: MSLs systematically uncover barriers that prevent optimal patient care, including insurance coverage limitations, prior authorization requirements, formulary restrictions, administration complexities, and cost considerations that affect treatment decisions. Understanding these barriers enables companies to develop targeted solutions, support programs, and advocacy strategies that improve patient access to appropriate treatments.

Healthcare Provider Perspectives and Decision-Making Processes: Insights about provider attitudes toward different treatment options, their clinical decision-making processes, educational needs, and communication preferences help companies develop more effective engagement strategies, educational programs, and scientific communication approaches. Understanding how providers evaluate new treatments and integrate them into practice enables more effective product positioning and support strategies.

Emerging Trends and Future Healthcare Directions: MSLs identify early signals about evolving treatment paradigms, emerging research areas, changing practice patterns, and shifts in healthcare delivery models that may impact future market dynamics and business opportunities. This forward-looking intelligence enables proactive strategic planning and competitive positioning.

STRATEGIC IMPACT OF MEDICAL INSIGHTS

Clinical Development Optimization: Medical insights inform clinical trial design by revealing real-world patient populations, identifying clinical endpoints that matter to practicing providers, highlighting protocol feasibility considerations, and anticipating potential recruitment challenges. This intelligence can significantly improve trial success rates, reduce development timelines, and enhance the clinical relevance of research programs.

Regulatory Strategy Enhancement: Understanding clinical practice patterns, safety considerations, and provider perspectives helps companies develop more compelling regulatory submissions and anticipate regulatory questions or concerns. Real-world evidence gathered through MSL interactions increasingly supports regulatory decision-making processes and can strengthen approval strategies.

Commercial Strategy Development: Insights about how products are used in practice, what drives provider preferences, and where competitive advantages exist enable companies to develop more effective positioning strategies, educational programs, and market access approaches. Understanding real-world treatment patterns informs commercial messaging and promotional strategy development.

Pipeline Prioritization and Innovation Strategy: Better understanding of unmet medical needs, treatment gaps, and provider frustrations with current therapeutic options helps companies prioritize research investments and identify the most promising development opportunities. These insights can influence portfolio decisions and resource allocation strategies.

Market Access and Health Economics: Insights about cost considerations, outcome measures that matter to providers and payers, and real-world effectiveness data support health economic arguments and payer negotiation strategies. MSLs often identify outcome measures and data needs that inform health economics research priorities and value demonstration strategies.

Product Lifecycle Management: Medical insights help companies optimize product positioning throughout the lifecycle, identify opportunities for label expansions, understand generic competition impact, and develop strategies for maintaining market position as products mature. This intelligence supports long-term brand management and lifecycle extension strategies.

The systematic gathering, analysis, and application of medical insights represents one of the most strategically valuable contributions MSLs make to their organizations. Success in this area requires not only strong relationship-building skills and scientific expertise, but also strategic thinking ability, pattern recognition skills, and the business acumen to translate field observations into actionable recommendations that drive organizational success while advancing patient care.

WHAT THEY DON'T TELL YOU: THE DAILY CHALLENGES OF MSL LIFE

Without question, the MSL role offers extraordinary opportunities to bridge cutting-edge science with clinical practice, creating meaningful impact on patient care through evidence-based education and strategic relationship building. However, the reality of MSL work extends far beyond the stimulating scientific discussions and conference presentations that initially attract many professionals to the field. Success demands considerable persistence in managing administrative complexities that underpin every strategic initiative—sending dozens of carefully crafted emails to healthcare providers who may never respond, spending substantial time documenting field activities and recording stakeholder insights, and navigating operational demands like researching compliant venues for educational programs or coordinating complex advisory board logistics.

The travel requirements and professional isolation present equally significant challenges. You'll spend countless hours driving between appointments, often for brief interactions with extraordinarily busy clinicians who may only have a distracted moment between patients. Extended periods away from family, missing important personal events, and managing the solitude of working independently across vast territories can create emotional strain. Perhaps most challenging are the inevitable periods when working alone for days triggers self-doubt about career choices and whether the impact justifies the personal sacrifices required.

During these difficult periods, successful MSLs return to their fundamental motivation—their "why"—that drove their transition into medical affairs while implementing strategic time management approaches that prevent burnout. The most resilient MSLs learn to find satisfaction in incremental progress, celebrate small victories in relationship building, and maintain focus on the long-term patient impact that results from their persistent efforts to advance scientific knowledge and evidence-based practice. Understanding that these challenges are inherent to the role enables MSLs to develop effective coping strategies and maintain perspective during inevitable difficult periods.

INTEGRATING CORE RESPONSIBILITIES

The core responsibilities of the MSL—scientific exchange, relationship building, conference engagement, and insight generation—represent far more than isolated tasks; they form an integrated strategic framework that amplifies impact through synergistic execution. Each responsibility reinforces and enhances the others: strong relationships enable more meaningful scientific exchanges, authentic scientific dialogue generates valuable insights that inform organizational strategy, conference interactions deepen existing relationships while creating new collaboration opportunities, and the intelligence gathered through all these activities positions MSLs as indispensable strategic assets within their organizations. This integrated approach distinguishes exceptional MSLs from their peers, as they understand that their ultimate success is measured not by the volume of activities completed, but by the quality of relationships built, the depth of insights generated, and the tangible impact on patient care that emerges from their strategic scientific influence.

When executed with authenticity, scientific rigor, and genuine commitment to advancing healthcare, these core responsibilities transform MSLs from information providers into trusted scientific partners whose work creates ripple effects throughout the healthcare ecosystem. The MSLs who master this integration become the bridge between cutting-edge research and real-world clinical practice, ensuring that scientific advances reach the patients who need them most while building careers that offer both intellectual fulfillment and meaningful contribution to human health. In this dynamic environment, the convergence of these responsibilities creates opportunities for MSLs to shape treatment paradigms, influence clinical practice, and ultimately leave a lasting legacy in the advancement of medical knowledge and patient care.

CHAPTER 2 TAKEAWAYS: CORE RESPONSIBILITY MASTERY

Scientific Exchange Excellence

- Can you conduct value-driven scientific exchanges that educate rather than promote?
- Do you understand how to prepare customized content for different stakeholder expertise levels?
- Have you mastered fair and balanced communication of clinical data?

Relationship Building Proficiency

- Can you identify and align with KOL professional objectives effectively?

- Do you understand how to balance personal connection with professional boundaries?
- Have you developed authentic, consistent approaches to relationship development?

Conference Strategy Optimization

- Can you develop comprehensive conference plans that maximize strategic value?
- Do you understand how to balance multiple conference responsibilities effectively?
- Have you identified approaches to leverage conferences for career advancement?

Medical Insights Generation

- Can you recognize and capture actionable intelligence from stakeholder interactions?
- Do you understand the strategic value different types of insights provide to your organization?
- Have you developed systematic approaches to insight synthesis and communication?

From Aspiration to Application 3

Mastering the MSL Job Search

"The skills you develop during your job search—researching stakeholder backgrounds, preparing thoughtful questions, listening actively, and following up professionally—directly transfer to the capabilities you'll need to excel as an MSL. View your job search not as a hurdle to overcome, but as preparation for the relationship-building excellence that defines successful medical science liaisons."

The journey from aspiring MSL to successful placement begins long before you submit your first application. It starts with a fundamental understanding of who you are as a professional, what drives your passion for healthcare, and how your unique background positions you for success in this dynamic field. This chapter will guide you through the critical process of self-assessment, strategic job searching, and the networking approaches that transform applications from resume submissions into meaningful conversations with hiring decision-makers.

THE FOUNDATION: DEEP SELF-REFLECTION AND CAREER ALIGNMENT

When charting your course into industry as an MSL, take time for deep self-reflection to evaluate your unique strengths, interests, and the driving forces that will sustain you through this career transition. This introspective process goes beyond simply cataloging your credentials—it requires honest

DOI: 10.1201/9781003781547-3

assessment of what truly energizes you professionally and personally. The MSL role demands passion and authenticity, qualities that cannot be faked during interviews or sustained over the long term without genuine motivation.

Discovering Your Therapeutic Area Passion

Examine the deeper motivations that fuel your passion for healthcare and scientific advancement. What diseases or patient populations have touched your heart or captured your intellectual curiosity? Perhaps you've witnessed firsthand the devastating impact of rare diseases on families and experienced the frustration of having limited therapeutic options to offer patients facing life-altering diagnoses. Maybe you've been inspired by breakthrough research in oncology or neurology, recognizing the transformative potential of precision medicine approaches. Or you've discovered significant gaps in care delivery that you're determined to help bridge through better education and evidence-based practice.

Consider the patient stories that have stayed with you long after your shifts ended, the research findings that excited you enough to share with colleagues over coffee, or the clinical challenges that kept you awake at night searching for solutions. These emotional touchstones often reveal your authentic areas of passion and can guide you toward therapeutic areas where your work will feel meaningful rather than merely transactional. When you align your career with causes that genuinely matter to you, the inevitable challenges of learning a new role become stepping stones rather than obstacles.

The most successful MSLs bring genuine enthusiasm to their work that extends beyond professional obligation. They can speak passionately about their therapeutic area not because they've memorized talking points, but because they truly care about the patients affected by these conditions. This authenticity resonates with healthcare providers who can immediately distinguish between scripted product knowledge and genuine scientific passion.

Identifying Your Professional Differentiators

Ask yourself probing questions that reveal your professional identity: what aspects of your scientific or clinical experience genuinely distinguish you from other candidates? Is it your ability to translate complex research into practical applications that clinicians can immediately implement? Your natural talent for building trust with diverse stakeholders across different professional cultures? Your analytical mind that consistently identifies patterns and connections that others miss? These differentiating strengths will become your professional signature and the foundation of your value proposition as an MSL.

Consider the moments in your career when you felt most engaged and effective. Perhaps you excelled at explaining complex pathophysiology to medical students, suggesting an aptitude for scientific education that's central to the MSL role. Maybe you found yourself naturally gravitating toward interdisciplinary team meetings where you could bridge communication gaps between different specialties—a skill directly applicable to cross-functional collaboration in pharmaceutical companies. These authentic strengths, when clearly articulated and strategically positioned during an interview, become the compelling narrative that sets you apart from hundreds of other qualified candidates.

Practical Career Considerations

This comprehensive self-assessment should also extend to practical considerations about your preferred work environment, lifestyle, and definition of professional fulfillment. The MSL role offers various configurations that can significantly impact your daily experience and long-term satisfaction. Are you energized by having greater autonomy as part of a small team with extensive travel within a large territory, where you might fly or have extensive drives regularly but enjoy significant independence in managing your schedule? Or do you prefer to be part of a larger team with a smaller, more focused territory that allows for deeper relationships but may involve more structured coordination and oversight?

Consider your family situation and lifestyle preferences honestly. The reality of MSL work includes substantial travel, often 50%–80% depending on territory size and company expectations. Some MSLs thrive on the variety and energy of constant travel, while others find the lifestyle challenging after several years. Understanding your preferences now will help you target opportunities that align with your personal and professional sustainability.

Do you want to work with established pharmaceutical companies with proven products and structured career advancement paths, or are you drawn to innovative biotech organizations developing cutting-edge therapies where you might have broader responsibilities but less defined hierarchies? Each environment offers distinct advantages and challenges, and your personality, risk tolerance, and career goals should inform this decision.

Take inventory of your existing professional network and relationships within specific therapeutic areas, as these often provide natural entry points where your background will be immediately valued. An APP practicing in cardiology considering an MSL transition might naturally gravitate toward cardiovascular therapeutic areas where their clinical credibility and existing relationships create immediate value. However, don't let existing networks limit your exploration—sometimes the most rewarding career moves involve expanding into new areas where your unique perspective brings fresh insights. Securing a foot in the door with a year's worth of MSL experience can afford you the ability to switch therapeutic areas with relative ease. Many successful MSLs find that their first role serves as a launching pad that opens doors to opportunities in their preferred therapeutic areas that may not have been accessible as a complete newcomer to the field.

When your career transition is grounded in genuine self-awareness and aligned with your true motivations, you'll not only be more successful in securing the right opportunity—you'll also find greater satisfaction and impact in the work itself. Remember, the most successful MSLs are those who bring genuine passion to their therapeutic areas, authentic enthusiasm for their work, and unwavering commitment to the patient populations they serve.

THE HARSH REALITY OF MSL JOB COMPETITION

You've completed this essential self-work and identified roles you want to pursue. Now comes the challenge of standing out in an intensely competitive market. MSL job requisitions can receive hundreds of applicants ranging from individuals with no prior industry experience to seasoned MSLs seeking new opportunities. This competition has intensified as the role's attractiveness has grown, with more healthcare professionals recognizing the MSL position as an ideal bridge between clinical practice and pharmaceutical innovation.

Understanding the Competitive Landscape

The requirements for MSL positions are typically consistent across companies, requiring a terminal degree (PhD, PharmD, MD) or extensive clinical experience in the therapeutic area of interest as an advanced practice provider. However, meeting these baseline qualifications merely grants you entry to the competition—it doesn't distinguish you from the hundreds of other qualified candidates applying for the same position.

Consider the daunting mathematics: a single MSL posting might attract 200+ applicants, with perhaps 20–30 receiving initial phone screenings, 8–12 advancing to formal interviews, 3–5 giving final a presentation and ultimately one candidate receiving an offer. These odds make the traditional "spray and pray" approach—submitting generic applications to multiple positions without strategic differentiation—largely ineffective for landing your first MSL role.

The challenge intensifies when you consider that hiring managers often prefer candidates with direct MSL or pharmaceutical industry experience. This creates a classic catch-22: you need MSL experience to get an MSL role, but you need an MSL role to gain MSL experience. However, understanding this dynamic allows you to develop strategies that circumvent this barrier through relationship building and authentic networking.

The Limitations of Blind Applications

Applying blindly without prior MSL experience feels like shooting your application off into space. While it's possible to receive an interview through this method, the probability remains discouragingly low. More likely, you'll receive the dreaded "thanks but no thanks" email, or even more frustrating, never hear back at all despite your qualifications and genuine interest.

In an age where artificial intelligence increasingly screens initial applications, your carefully crafted resume might never reach human eyes if it doesn't contain the precise keywords and experience patterns the algorithms are programmed to identify. Taking the proactive step to identify and contact the human decision-makers enables you to bypass this digital screening process and ensures your candidacy receives real consideration.

The most successful career transitioners understand that the job search process is fundamentally about building relationships and creating advocates who can support your candidacy internally. Your resume becomes a conversation starter rather than a standalone pitch, and your networking efforts transform you from an anonymous applicant into a known quantity with internal supporters.

STRATEGIC NETWORKING: THE FOUNDATION OF MSL SUCCESS

Much like the MSL role itself, networking represents the most critical component of landing your first MSL position, yet it's often the area where aspiring MSLs feel most uncomfortable or uncertain. Many healthcare professionals, particularly those with academic or clinical backgrounds, may feel awkward about what they perceive as "selling themselves" or building relationships for professional advancement disingenuously. However, effective MSL networking isn't about self-promotion—it's about building genuine professional relationships based on mutual value creation and shared interest in advancing patient care.

LinkedIn: Your Primary Networking Platform

LinkedIn serves as your most powerful networking tool and professional presence platform. If you can afford it, LinkedIn Premium provides significant advantages for your MSL job search by enabling unlimited messaging to professionals outside your network, advanced search capabilities, and insights about who's viewing your profile. Consider this a short-term investment in your career transition—the cost of Premium membership pales in comparison to the salary increase you'll achieve by landing an MSL role.

Optimize your LinkedIn profile specifically for MSL opportunities by incorporating relevant keywords, highlighting transferable skills, and clearly articulating your career transition goals. Your headline should reflect your MSL aspirations rather than just your current role, and your summary should tell the story of why you're pursuing medical affairs and what unique value you'll bring to the field.

Creating Internal Advocates

After identifying a prospective role, your next step involves comprehensive stakeholder research to identify the key decision-makers and influencers in the hiring process. This research typically reveals three categories of crucial contacts:

Current Team MSLs represent your most valuable networking targets because they possess insider knowledge about the role, team dynamics, territorial challenges, and company culture. They can provide insights that no job description captures and often serve as informal screeners for potential candidates. Understanding the makeup of the existing team and the specific characteristics the hiring manager is looking for in a candidate will inform how you approach contacting and communicating with the hiring manager.

The Hiring Manager typically isn't named in job postings but can often be identified through LinkedIn research, company websites, or identified from your conversation with the current team member. This person makes the final hiring decision and represents the ultimate relationship to cultivate.

The Recruiter is usually identified in the job posting and serves as the formal gateway to the application process. However, approaching recruiters after establishing relationships with team members positions you as a referred candidate rather than a cold applicant.

Informational Interview Excellence

Set up time to have virtual meetings or phone calls with current MSLs with the primary objective of better understanding their team and the role you're considering. Approach these conversations like seeking answers to a test from someone who's already taken it—a mindset that positions you as a learner rather than a seller.

Prepare thoughtful questions that demonstrate your interest while gathering valuable intelligence: ask about territory size and geographic coverage, typical travel requirements and schedule flexibility, current challenges they face in the role and solutions they've implemented to overcome these obstacles. Inquire about company culture, team dynamics, and their relationship with the hiring manager. Understand how MSLs are evaluated for productivity (i.e. metrics and impacts) and what success looks like in their organization.

Most importantly, initially focus on being curious about their experience rather than promoting your own background and expertise. This approach builds rapport and demonstrates the kind of genuine interest and listening skills that make excellent MSLs. When the conversation naturally returns to your background—and it will—be prepared to deliver a concise 30-second elevator pitch explaining why you're a suitable candidate with 2–3 specific, compelling reasons. You may leverage your scientific background or passion for a specific patient population. Whatever the reason, be authentic and to the point.

The MSL Job Networking Workaid provided at the end of this book will help guide you through mapping these important relationships.

The Internal Referral Strategy

At the conclusion of these informational interviews, thank them for their time and insights. If the conversation went well and you remain interested in the role, make two strategic requests: ask if they'd be willing to review your resume and provide feedback, and inquire whether they'd be comfortable providing an internal referral for the position.

This request might seem presumptuous after a single conversation, but internal referral bonuses can be more than $2,000, making current employees financially motivated to help qualified candidates. More importantly, MSLs understand the challenges of breaking into the field and often want to support promising candidates who demonstrate genuine passion and preparation.

An internal referral transforms your application from one of hundreds to a priority candidate. When you subsequently reach out to the recruiter and hiring manager, you can reference your positive conversation with their team member, mention that you've applied with an internal referral, and request time to discuss how your background aligns with their needs.

RESUME CUSTOMIZATION: CRAFTING YOUR STRATEGIC NARRATIVE

The art of resume customization extends far beyond simply rearranging bullet points—it requires thoughtful transformation of your professional narrative to align with the target opportunity. Your resume must speak the language of both the specific therapeutic area and the individual company's culture and priorities, demonstrating that you understand not just the role requirements but the strategic context in which you'll be operating. Still, your resume should remain succinct—one to two pages maximum—requiring disciplined curation of your professional accomplishments.

Rather than overwhelming hiring managers with an exhaustive catalog of your 30+ publications and presentations, select the one or two most impactful examples that best tell your story and directly relate to the role you're pursuing. This selective approach demonstrates strategic thinking and respect for the reader's time while highlighting your most relevant credentials. For comprehensive documentation of your scholarly work, include a brief note directing readers to your complete publication record—whether through a personal website, LinkedIn profile, or by simply stating "Complete publication list available upon request." Remember, your resume serves as a compelling introduction that should leave hiring managers wanting to learn more about your background, not as an exhaustive academic curriculum vitae that attempts to document every professional achievement.

Mastering Therapeutic Area Languages

How you articulate and present your experience should mirror not only the language used in the job posting itself but also the terminology, priorities, and competencies that define success in that specific therapeutic area. Study each job description like a scientific manuscript, identifying key phrases such as "stakeholder engagement," "clinical insights generation," "launch excellence," or "real-world evidence." Weave these terms naturally into your accomplishments and role descriptions, demonstrating that you understand the strategic priorities and communication norms of the field.

This strategic approach demands that you become fluent in multiple therapeutic vocabularies. Say for example you are applying for an MSL role that supports an anticoagulation therapeutic, but your background is in respiratory care. Your respiratory experience treating COPD patients can be reframed to highlight your expertise in managing complex, chronic conditions requiring careful medication monitoring—skills directly relevant to anticoagulation management where dosing precision and patient adherence monitoring are critical. Your familiarity with inhaled therapies translates to understanding of specialized drug delivery systems and the patient adherence challenges that affect treatment outcomes across therapeutic areas.

The clinical decision-making skills you developed in respiratory care demonstrate the analytical thinking essential for any MSL role, regardless of therapeutic focus. Your experience interpreting pulmonary function tests, analyzing treatment response patterns, and adjusting therapeutic regimens based on patient-specific factors showcases the scientific rigor and clinical judgment that MSLs need when discussing complex clinical scenarios with healthcare providers.

Developing Your Resume Portfolio Strategy

It may take several iterations and considerable time investment, but eventually you'll develop a portfolio of effective resume versions, each laser-focused on specific therapeutic areas or company types you're targeting. This strategic approach requires creating a master document containing all your experiences, achievements, publications, and skills, then crafting specialized versions that emphasize different aspects of your background.

Your oncology-focused resume may highlight different research projects, publications, and clinical experiences than your rare disease version, even though both draw from the same career foundation. The oncology version might emphasize your experience with complex treatment protocols, multidisciplinary care coordination, and patient advocacy during difficult treatment journeys. Your rare disease version might focus on diagnostic challenges, patient and family education, advocacy, and collaboration with specialized centers and support organizations.

Company-Specific Customization

Remember that this customization process extends beyond therapeutic areas to company characteristics and organizational cultures. A startup biotech values different experiences and competencies than an established pharmaceutical giant. The entrepreneurial problem-solving you demonstrated during resource-constrained academic research may resonate strongly with a nimble biotech company where MSLs wear multiple hats and contribute to diverse projects. Your experience navigating complex healthcare systems and building relationships across large institutions might appeal more to a large pharmaceutical company managing multiple stakeholder relationships and formal processes.

Each resume version should tell a coherent, compelling story about why your unique background makes you the ideal candidate for that specific opportunity, leaving no doubt in the hiring manager's mind that you understand both the role requirements and the therapeutic landscape you're entering. This level of customization demonstrates the strategic thinking and attention to detail that characterize successful MSLs.

BUILDING RELATIONSHIPS WITH RECRUITMENT PROFESSIONALS

Another valuable resource to assist you in your hiring journey includes recruiters from specialized pharmaceutical recruitment agencies. These professionals possess deep industry knowledge, extensive networks, and insights about market trends that can significantly accelerate your job search while helping you avoid common pitfalls.

Proactive Recruiter Engagement

You can proactively reach out to recruiters even in the absence of specific openings, focusing on building relationships and refining your search strategy. During an introductory call with a recruiter, they will evaluate many of the characteristics you explored during your initial self-assessment, getting to know you as a person and identifying which opportunities represent good fits for both their company clients and your career goals.

Experienced pharmaceutical recruiters can provide valuable feedback on your resume, interview skills, and market positioning. They understand what different companies prioritize in MSL candidates and can help you identify areas for improvement or additional preparation. This guidance often proves invaluable for candidates making their first transition into pharmaceutical roles.

Long-term Relationship Value

While opportunities sourced by hiring agencies for brand new MSLs are relatively rare, they do exist, particularly with smaller biotech companies or specialty pharmaceutical organizations that source contract positions. Regardless of whether they have immediate opportunities, the relationship represents long-term career value that extends well beyond your first MSL role.

Recruiters who know your background and capabilities will reach out when appropriate opportunities become available. More importantly, if you eventually find yourself between roles due to layoffs, company reorganizations, or career transitions, you'll immediately have advocates who understand your strengths and can quickly connect you with new opportunities.

As you build your professional network, remember that everyone represents a potential customer or partner. Although a recruiter may not have opportunities in your preferred territory, you may know strong candidates in other regions where they do have openings. Building rapport and maintaining these relationships keeps you top of mind as recruiters continue to source candidates for their clients, creating a network effect that expands your opportunities over time.

Strategic Communication with All Stakeholders

As soon as you begin any communications with recruiters, hiring managers, or team members, treat every interaction as though it's part of your interview process. In many ways, it is. These professionals are evaluating not just your qualifications, but your communication style, professionalism, reliability, and cultural fit throughout every exchange.

Be genuine, thorough, respectful, and complete in all your communications. Respond promptly to emails and phone calls, follow through on commitments, and maintain the same level of professionalism you would demonstrate in formal interview settings. This approach often distinguishes you from other candidates and might be the factor that lands you a formal interview opportunity.

CONCLUSION: INTEGRATING STRATEGY WITH AUTHENTICITY

The journey from aspiring MSL to successful placement requires careful integration of strategic thinking with authentic relationship building. Your success depends not just on meeting qualifications or networking effectively, but on finding the intersection where your genuine passions, unique strengths, and market opportunities align.

The most successful MSL candidates understand that this process requires patience, relentless persistence, and genuine commitment to building relationships rather than simply collecting contacts. They approach each conversation with curiosity and respect, recognizing that today's informational interview contact might become tomorrow's colleague, collaborator, or advocate.

Remember that the MSL role itself centers on relationship building and authentic communication with healthcare stakeholders. The skills you develop during your job search—researching stakeholder backgrounds, preparing thoughtful questions, listening actively, and following up professionally—directly transfer to the capabilities you'll need to excel as an MSL. View your job search not as a hurdle to overcome, but as preparation for the relationship-building excellence that defines successful medical science liaisons.

In the next chapter, we'll explore how to excel in MSL interviews, transforming the relationships and insights you've developed through strategic networking into compelling conversations that demonstrate your readiness to contribute immediately to your new role and organization.

CHAPTER 3 TAKEAWAYS: STRATEGIC JOB SEARCH MASTERY

Self-Assessment Excellence

- Have you completed comprehensive self-reflection to identify your unique professional differentiators?
- Can you articulate your authentic passion for specific therapeutic areas or patient populations?
- Do you understand your preferred work environment and lifestyle considerations?

Networking Strategy Implementation

- Have you optimized your LinkedIn profile for MSL opportunities and considered Premium membership?
- Can you systematically identify and research key stakeholders for target roles?
- [Have you developed skills for conducting effective informational interviews?

Application Excellence

- Do you understand the competitive landscape and limitations of blind applications?
- Have you developed a portfolio approach to resume customization for different opportunities?
- Can you adapt your professional narrative to align with specific therapeutic areas and company cultures?

Relationship-Building Proficiency

- Have you identified and begun building relationships with pharmaceutical recruiters?
- Do you understand how to leverage internal referrals to transform your candidacy?
- Can you maintain professional communication standards throughout the job search process?

MSL Interview Mastery

4

From First Call to Final Offer

Congratulations! You've received the call from HR about your dream Medical Science Liaison (MSL) role. This moment represents the culmination of your strategic networking efforts and the beginning of a structured evaluation process that will determine whether you join the ranks of medical science liaisons. Whether you realize it or not, your interview process has already begun with the first impressions you made during your informational meeting with the current MSL team member, your conversations with the recruiter, and your initial outreach to the hiring manager.

Understanding that these preliminary interactions serve as informal screening stages is crucial for maintaining consistency and professionalism throughout the entire process. The formal interview journey typically unfolds in a predictable sequence: an initial screening call with HR, a comprehensive discussion with the hiring manager, a cultural fit assessment with current team members, and a final panel presentation that demonstrates your scientific communication capabilities and strategic thinking.

While this roadmap may seem daunting when laid out in its entirety, breaking down each component and understanding the specific objectives for every interaction will transform what could feel overwhelming into a strategic, manageable process where you can excel by thorough preparation and authentic engagement.

DOI: 10.1201/9781003781547-4

PHASE ONE: THE HR SCREENING CALL—ESTABLISHING FOUNDATION AND FIT

During your initial call with the HR representative, you're undergoing a multifaceted evaluation that extends beyond basic qualification verification. They're assessing your communication style, cultural fit potential, financial alignment, and most importantly, the authenticity and depth of your motivation for pursuing this specific MSL role.

Articulating Your "Why" with Conviction

The most critical element of this conversation centers on your ability to articulate why you're applying for **this** particular MSL role with genuine conviction and specific knowledge. Your response should demonstrate thorough research and authentic connection to the opportunity rather than generic enthusiasm for any MSL position.

Is it something specific about the company that excites you, such as their innovative pipeline that distinguishes them from competitors in meaningful ways? Perhaps you're drawn to their commitment to rare diseases, their cutting-edge gene therapy approaches, or their patient-centric development philosophy that aligns with your values. Maybe it's the specific therapeutic area that ignites your passion and where you're eager to make a tangible impact in advancing clinical care based on your professional experience and personal motivation.

Conducting comprehensive homework about the company's pipeline, competitive positioning, and strategic direction demonstrates both your commitment to the interview process and your naturally detail-oriented approach to professional challenges. This preparation should include understanding recent clinical trial results, regulatory milestones, competitive advantages, and market opportunities that position the company for success.

Salary Expectations: Positioning Yourself Strategically

The HR representative will inevitably ask about your salary expectations, a moment that requires careful preparation and strategic positioning. It's essential to conduct thorough research based on current industry standards rather than limiting yourself based on your current compensation, particularly if you're transitioning from academic or clinical roles with traditionally lower compensation structures.

Many candidates make the critical error of anchoring their expectations to their current salary rather than market value for MSL roles. For example, a postdoctoral researcher earning $50,000 annually might initially feel grateful for any salary above $90,000–$100,000, not realizing that entry-level MSL positions typically range from $140,000–$155,000 in base salary, plus performance bonuses (typically 10%–20% of base), car allowances ($600–$800 monthly), and long-term equity incentives.

According to the 2024 Annual Medical Science Liaison Society Salary Survey, MSLs with 1 year of experience or less average a base salary of about $167,000. The full survey provides excellent benchmarking data as your career progresses and you gain more years of experience. Additionally, these compensation data are broken down by experience level, therapeutic area, company type, and geographic region. Position your unique expertise, years of relevant experience, and specialized knowledge to justify placement at the upper end of the appropriate range.

When discussing salary expectations, maintain confidence while demonstrating market awareness: "Based on industry standards and my background in [specific expertise area], I believe a base salary in the range of $X is appropriate for this role." Don't belabor the point or provide extensive justification—simply state your expectations clearly and move on. The HR representative is primarily determining whether your expectations fall within their budgeted range rather than negotiating specifics at this stage. They may even volunteer their approved range.

Communication Excellence and Follow-Through

Your communication style during this call provides valuable insight into how you'll interact with healthcare providers, internal stakeholders, and cross-functional team members. Demonstrate the same professionalism, clarity, and engagement that you'll bring to KOL interactions by listening actively, asking thoughtful questions, and providing complete, well-organized responses.

PHASE TWO: THE HIRING MANAGER—ARTICULATING YOUR VALUE PROPOSITION

Congratulations! The HR representative found you to be a compelling candidate and wants to schedule time with the hiring manager. Don't delay in responding—accommodate their schedule to the best of your ability and strike while the iron is hot. Be prompt and clear in your communication and availability to advance to the next step. You want to remain top of mind and limit opportunities for other candidates to gain momentum.

Crafting Your Professional Narrative

In your conversation with the hiring manager, be prepared to provide a concise but compelling overview of your resume and experience. However, avoid simply reading your credentials verbatim. A major component of medical affairs and MSL work involves creating coherent scientific narratives and communicating them effectively to diverse audiences.

Transform your resume into a compelling story that demonstrates why you've inevitably concluded that this specific MSL role at this particular company represents the ideal next step in your career trajectory. Your narrative should weave together your educational background, professional experiences, research accomplishments, and personal motivations into a coherent explanation of your career evolution and future aspirations.

Come prepared with specific, detailed stories that demonstrate key characteristics hiring managers seek: intellectual curiosity, professional humility, ability to learn quickly, capacity to receive and integrate coaching, and collaborative leadership skills. If you have pre-existing relationships with thought leaders in your geographic territory or therapeutic area, emphasize these connections as valuable assets you bring to the role.

The Character Assessment Through Behavioral Examples

Hiring managers understand they won't find perfect candidates who possess every desired qualification and skill. What they seek are professionals who will have a short learning curve and can make positive impact quickly while growing into the full scope of the role over time.

Prepare concrete examples that illustrate:

Problem-Solving Capability: Describe situations where you identified complex challenges and developed creative, effective solutions that required collaboration across different stakeholders or disciplines.

Learning Agility: Share examples of rapidly mastering new concepts, techniques, or responsibilities when transitioning between roles, projects, or therapeutic areas.

Relationship Building: Provide specific instances where you developed productive professional relationships with challenging personalities or across different organizational cultures.

Scientific Communication: Detail experiences translating complex research findings or clinical concepts for audiences with varying levels of expertise and technical background.

Resilience and Adaptability: Discuss how you've navigated significant changes, setbacks, or unexpected challenges while maintaining productivity and positive attitude.

Cultural Fit: The Unwritten but Critical Requirement

One of the most important characteristics hiring managers evaluate—though it's rarely explicitly stated in job descriptions—is fit with the existing team culture and organizational values. You could possess extraordinary credentials, extensive KOL networks, and impressive research backgrounds, but if you don't demonstrate humility and present yourself as someone who will compliment team dynamics, you won't receive an offer.

This cultural assessment occurs throughout your interactions, but particularly during conversations with current team members. Your ability to build natural rapport during your initial informational interview and any formal team interactions provides valuable data about how you'll integrate with colleagues and contribute to collaborative team success.

Demonstrate cultural fit by showing genuine interest in team members as professionals and individuals, asking thoughtful questions about their experiences and perspectives, and displaying the kind of collegial respect and intellectual humility that characterize effective MSL teams.

PHASE THREE: ASKING THE RIGHT QUESTIONS

In each interview conversation, you'll have opportunities to ask questions that further distinguish you as a thoughtful, prepared candidate who thinks strategically about professional opportunities and career development. The Workaid has a comprehensive set of questions for HR representatives, hiring managers, and current MSL team members for you to consider.

Questions for HR Representatives

Focus your HR questions on practical aspects of the role and organizational structure:

Territory and Travel Logistics: "Can you describe the geographic territory and typical travel expectations for this role? How does the company support MSLs in managing travel demands while maintaining work-life balance?"

Team Composition and Development: "What is the current size and composition of the MSL team? What professional development opportunities does the company provide for medical affairs professionals?"

Success Metrics and Evaluation: "How do you typically measure MSL success, and what does the performance evaluation process look like?"

Organizational Growth: "What does career progression typically look like within medical affairs, and how does the company support professional advancement?"

Avoid overly technical scientific questions with HR representatives, as they typically lack the therapeutic area expertise to engage meaningfully on these topics. Similarly, avoid proactively raising detailed questions about benefits and compensation until they introduce these topics, maintaining focus on the role and organizational opportunity rather than appearing primarily motivated by financial considerations.

Questions for Hiring Managers

Your questions for hiring managers should demonstrate strategic thinking and long-term commitment:

Performance Expectations and Metrics: "How will you measure my success in this role during the first 30 days, 90 days, and first year? What does excellence look like for MSLs on your team?"

Strategic Direction: "What are you most excited about regarding the company's direction and the medical affairs team's role in that growth? What opportunities do you see emerging in this therapeutic area?"

Ideal Candidate Profile: "From a cultural and collaborative standpoint, what characteristics define your most successful team members? How do you prefer to work with your MSLs?"

Professional Development: "How does the medical affairs organization support career development and advancement? What growth opportunities exist for high-performing MSLs?"

Current Challenges and Opportunities: "What are the biggest challenges and opportunities facing the medical affairs team currently? How would this role contribute to addressing those priorities?"

These questions demonstrate your strategic thinking, long-term commitment, and understanding that MSL success requires both individual excellence and team collaboration.

Questions for Current Team Members

When interacting with current MSLs, focus on authentic relationship building and practical insights:

Day-to-Day Realities: "What does a typical week look like for you? What aspects of the role do you find most rewarding and most challenging?"

Professional Growth: "How has your own career developed since joining this team? What learning opportunities have been most valuable for your development?"

Team Dynamics: "How would you describe the collaborative culture within the medical affairs team? How do team members support each other's success?"

Work-Life Integration: "How do you manage the travel requirements and maintain personal relationships and interests outside of work?"

Strategic Perspective: "What developments in this therapeutic area or within the company are you most excited about for the future?"

These questions demonstrate genuine interest in team members as professionals and individuals while gathering valuable intelligence about the actual role experience rather than idealized job descriptions. A comprehensive list of question ideas with different intent is included in the appendix. Find the ones that resonate with you most, or use them as a springboard for your own.

PHASE FOUR: THE PANEL PRESENTATION—DEMONSTRATING MSL READINESS

Congratulations! You've advanced to the panel interview stage, which represents the final and most comprehensive evaluation of your MSL readiness. This session typically occurs either in-person or virtually and involves both a formal presentation and behavioral interview questioning. While the sequence may vary, you should prepare thoroughly for both components as they assess different but equally important competencies.

Presentation Preparation and Delivery Excellence

During the presentation component, evaluators assess your scientific storytelling abilities and communication style as if you were conducting a scientific exchange with KOLs. This evaluation encompasses content organization, slide design, delivery confidence, audience engagement, and ability to handle questions under pressure.

Pre-Presentation Setup: Before beginning your presentation, communicate your preference for handling questions. You might say, "I'm comfortable taking questions throughout the presentation as they arise, as I find this creates more engaging dialogue," or "I'd prefer to hold questions until the end so I can maintain the flow of the scientific narrative." This demonstrates professional presentation experience and consideration for audience preferences.

Storytelling Structure: When creating your presentation, you might follow the classic communication framework: tell them what you're going to tell them, tell them, and then tell them what you've told them. This structure ensures clarity and reinforces key messages while maintaining audience engagement throughout the presentation.

As a scientist or clinician, you may naturally gravitate toward detailed methodology discussions or comprehensive patient experience descriptions. Instead, focus on ensuring each slide delivers a clear, concise takeaway that flows logically to the next concept and fits cohesively within the overarching narrative you're developing about the study results, therapeutic area landscape, or disease state education you're presenting.

Practice and Refinement: Practice your presentation extensively until the content flows naturally and confidently. You may want to begin with a scripted approach to develop verbal fluency with complex concepts, figure or graph orientation, and transitions between slides. The more you practice verbalizing the content, the more naturally it will flow during the actual presentation.

Don't worry about sounding too rehearsed—thorough preparation will make you sound polished and professional rather than scripted. On presentation day, it's perfectly acceptable to have notes available for reference, but avoid reading directly from scripts or slides. If presenting virtually, maintain engagement by looking directly at the camera (the small light at the top of your screen) as much as possible to simulate eye contact with panel members.

Behavioral Interview Mastery

Behavioral interview questions may initially seem challenging, but they become opportunities to shine with proper preparation and practice. These questions serve multiple evaluation purposes: assessing how you'll perform in complex MSL situations, understanding your thought processes and decision-making frameworks, and evaluating your emotional intelligence and interpersonal skills through analysis of your past behavior patterns. Consult the "MSL Behavioral Interview Questions and STAR Response Worksheet" to structure and practice your responses.

Understanding the Purpose: Behavioral questions operate on the premise that past behavior represents the best predictor of future performance. Rather than asking hypothetical questions like "How would you handle a difficult KOL?" they ask "Tell me about a time when you had to manage a challenging stakeholder relationship. What was the situation, what actions did you take, and what was the outcome?"

Strategic Preparation Approach: While it's impossible to prepare for every potential behavioral question, you can develop a strategic approach by identifying 8–10 compelling professional anecdotes that demonstrate different competencies and can be adapted to various question types. Assign a brief phrase or title to each that triggers the story.

For example, a story about publishing a research paper despite multiple rejections could address questions about:

- Handling failure or setbacks
- Persistence and resilience
- Learning from feedback
- Managing frustration or disappointment
- Collaborating with difficult reviewers or editors
- Problem-solving and adaptation

The STAR Method Framework: Structure your responses using the STAR method as following.

- **Situation:** Provide clear, concise context about the challenge or opportunity
- **Task:** Explain your specific role and responsibilities in the situation
- **Action:** Describe the specific actions you took, emphasizing your personal contributions
- **Result:** Share the outcomes achieved and lessons learned from the experience

Embracing Growth Through Challenges: It's not only acceptable but advantageous to discuss professional challenges, setbacks, or failures—provided you can articulate how these experiences contributed to your growth and development. For instance, you might describe how a research paper was rejected multiple times, but through integrating reviewer feedback and refining your approach, you eventually achieved publication in a peer-reviewed journal while becoming a stronger scientist, writer, and critical thinker.

Even if the final outcome wasn't your initial goal, you can demonstrate how the experience taught you to anticipate potential weaknesses in your work, integrate constructive feedback effectively, and approach future projects with enhanced strategic thinking.

Common Behavioral Question Categories and Preparation

Leadership and Influence: "Describe a time when you had to influence others without formal authority."

Problem-Solving: "Tell me about a complex problem you solved. Walk me through your approach."

Communication: "Give me an example of when you had to present complex information to an audience with varying levels of expertise."

Adaptability: "Describe a time when you had to quickly adapt to significant changes in your work environment or responsibilities."

Conflict Resolution: "Tell me about a time when you had to resolve a disagreement or conflict with a colleague or stakeholder."

Learning Agility: "Share an example of when you had to quickly master a new skill or knowledge area for your work."

For each category, prepare at least one detailed example that showcases your competency while demonstrating the strategic thinking and collaborative approach essential for MSL success. Take the time to work through the MSL Behavioral Interview Questions and STAR Response Worksheet and practice verbalizing your responses.

NEGOTIATING YOUR OFFER: SECURING THE BAG

Congratulations! You receive an offer. While you may be eager to sign on the dotted line, remember that negotiation represents a normal, expected part of the hiring process, even in specialized fields like medical affairs. Although there are times when there is no wiggle room, companies typically build flexibility into their initial offers, anticipating some level of discussion about terms and compensation.

Research-Based Negotiation Strategy

Before any negotiation conversation, make it clear that you are excited to join the team and new company. You never want to negotiate yourself out of an offer if it is truly a role you want. Still, arm yourself with current market data from reputable sources like the MSL Society salary surveys, PayScale, and industry-specific compensation reports. Understand the typical compensation structure for MSL roles, which typically includes base salary, performance bonuses, car allowances, stock options or equity participation, professional development budgets, and comprehensive benefits packages.

Areas of Negotiation

Base Salary: From a compensatory standpoint, base salary is your best opportunity to negotiate. If the offered base salary falls below market range for your experience level and geographic area, present your case using industry data and specific value proposition. "Based on industry benchmarks and my experience in [specific area], I was expecting a base salary closer to $X. Given my background in [specific expertise] and relationships with [relevant stakeholders], I believe this adjustment reflects appropriate market value."

Bonus Structure: Most bonus structures in medical affairs are given as some % of your base salary ranging from 13% to 20%. These are typically standardized across the company based on pay level and not subject to individualization. Nonetheless, managers can pay out above or below the given percentage, so it's critical to understand how performance is evaluated early in your tenure. If the standard % is on the low end of the range, that might be rationale to ask for small bump in the base salary.

Company Equity: In smaller companies, you may receive stock options or restricted stock units as part of your offer. If the company is precommercial, there could be tremendous financial upside in this component of the offer. Factor in potential growth for the company, what the stock may be worth in the future based on similar companies, the history of the executive leadership team, etc. Options tend to have more flexibility for negotiation.

Start Date and Transition Support: If you need additional time to wrap up current commitments or relocate, most companies can accommodate reasonable requests that demonstrate professionalism and responsibility.

Negotiation Approach and Tone

Approach negotiations professionally and collaboratively, emphasizing your enthusiasm for the role while ensuring fair compensation. "I'm very excited about this opportunity and believe I can make significant contributions to the team. I'd like to discuss a few aspects of the offer to ensure we're aligned on fair market compensation."

Express appreciation for the offer, present your research-based requests clearly, and remain open to alternative solutions. Sometimes companies cannot adjust base salary due to equity concerns but may increase signing bonuses, accelerate review timelines, or enhance professional development benefits. This negotiation sets the foundation for your initial compensation, which influences all future raises and career progression.

Bringing It All Together: Your Path to Interview Success

The MSL interview process represents far more than a series of conversations—it serves as a comprehensive evaluation of your readiness to excel in one of the pharmaceutical industry's most strategically important and relationship-dependent roles. Success requires integrating thorough preparation with authentic relationship building, demonstrating that the same qualities driving interview excellence will determine your effectiveness as an MSL.

Your ability to research company positioning, prepare compelling narratives, and handle complex behavioral questions directly translates to the analytical thinking and communication skills essential for territory management and stakeholder engagement. The curiosity you demonstrate about team dynamics and strategic direction mirrors the intellectual approach you'll need for building productive KOL relationships and generating valuable market insights.

Most importantly, treat every interaction—from initial informational interviews through final panel presentations—as an opportunity to build genuine relationships with future colleagues who may become collaborators, mentors, or advocates throughout your career. The authenticity and collaborative spirit you demonstrate during interviews directly reflect the professional qualities that distinguish exceptional MSLs from merely competent ones.

Whether you receive this particular offer or continue your search, approach every interview with relentless persistence and a learning mindset. Each conversation sharpens your self-presentation skills, deepens your understanding of medical affairs work, and expands your professional network. If an opportunity doesn't materialize, use the experience to refine your approach, strengthen your preparation, and maintain the determined pursuit that characterizes successful MSL candidates. It's not inappropriate to reach out to the hiring manager and schedule a 5-minute conversation to receive constructive feedback as to why you didn't receive the offer. To be clear, this is **not** an opportunity to tell them how they missed out on you or that you disagree with their decision. Reacting this way would only confirm their decision that you're not ready. Their decision is made, there is nothing you can do to change the outcome. What you can do is listen earnestly and respectfully and grow from the experience.

Remember that your transition into medical affairs represents an opportunity to amplify your impact on patient care through strategic scientific influence. The preparation, authenticity, and persistence you develop through this process will serve you throughout your MSL career, ensuring that your eventual success stems not from luck, but from the disciplined approach that defines excellence in medical science liaison work.

CHAPTER 4 TAKEAWAYS: INTERVIEW EXCELLENCE MASTERY

Preparation Excellence

- Have you developed a compelling professional narrative that connects your background to MSL work?
- Can you articulate your "why" for specific companies and therapeutic areas with authentic conviction?
- Have you researched industry-standard compensation and prepared for salary discussions?

Behavioral Interview Readiness

- Have you identified 8–10 compelling professional anecdotes that demonstrate key MSL competencies?
- Can you structure responses using the STAR method effectively?
- Are you prepared to discuss growth from challenges and setbacks authentically?

Presentation Skills

- Have you practiced delivering scientific presentations that balance detail with clear takeaways?
- Can you engage audiences effectively while handling questions professionally?
- Do you understand how to adapt communication style for diverse stakeholder groups?

Strategic Questioning

- Have you prepared thoughtful questions appropriate for each interview stage and stakeholder?
- Can you demonstrate long-term thinking and commitment through your inquiries?

- Do you understand how to build rapport while gathering valuable role insights?

Professional Excellence

- Are you prepared to negotiate offers professionally using market-based research?
- Can you maintain authentic relationships while advancing through the interview process?
- Do you understand how interview performance translates to MSL success competencies?

The AI Revolution in Medical Affairs 5

Regardless of whether you recently landed your dream job as a Medical Science Liaison (MSL) or are a seasoned veteran, medical affairs and the MSL role never stops evolving. Artificial intelligence (AI) will remodel the job market in many industries, but for the savvy learners, leveraging its power can be a differentiating skill. There are countless ways to leverage AI as an MSL to supercharge your productivity. If you can demonstrate your creativity using AI to support your excellence in the field either as a candidate or within your role, you may find yourself on the fast track to advancing in your career either through promotions or candidacy for future roles.

The modern MSL operates in an information-rich environment where staying current with scientific literature, maintaining meaningful relationships with key opinion leaders, and translating complex data into actionable insights are fundamental to success. Traditional approaches to these challenges—while still valuable—can be time-intensive and may not scale with the increasing volume of scientific information and stakeholder expectations.

Enter AI: a powerful set of technologies that can augment human capabilities, automate routine tasks, and uncover insights that might otherwise remain hidden in vast datasets. For MSLs, AI represents not a threat to job security, but an opportunity to elevate their impact and influence within the scientific community.

THE STRATEGIC IMPERATIVE FOR AI ADOPTION

AI can be seamlessly integrated into MSL workflows to enhance daily productivity and strategic impact. Immediate applications include literature monitoring and synthesis, scientific paper summarization, narrative development, competitive intelligence analysis, field insight transformation, email template

DOI: 10.1201/9781003781547-5

generation, and discussion guide creation for KOL meetings. While these tools offer significant efficiency gains, MSLs must apply strategic judgment to ensure AI outputs align with their objectives and company priorities—uncritical reliance on AI-generated content risks diluting focus from core strategic goals.

The most accessible entry points for AI adoption are routine information processing tasks that currently consume substantial time but don't require complex decision-making. However, successful integration requires deliberate planning to maximize benefits while preserving the critical thinking and relationship management skills that define MSL excellence. Developing proficiency with these technologies now provides competitive advantages in career advancement, enabling MSLs to demonstrate innovation leadership and comprehensive role mastery in interviews and internal discussions.

THE PRODUCTIVITY PARADOX

The most successful MSLs of the future will be those who can harness AI to handle routine information processing while focusing their human expertise on relationship building, strategic thinking, and complex problem-solving. This creates what we might call the "AI Amplification Effect"—where technology enhances human capabilities rather than replacing them.

Consider the typical MSL workflow: scanning dozens of publications weekly, preparing customized presentations for different audiences, tracking competitive developments, and synthesizing insights for internal teams. Each of these activities requires significant time investment, yet much of the initial information processing can be enhanced or streamlined through AI tools.

Synthesizing and Summarizing Literature

Being viewed as a scientific expert by our KOLs is challenging given the multitude of competing priorities of the MSL role. The volume of scientific literature published daily makes comprehensive monitoring nearly impossible through traditional methods. A typical therapeutic area might see dozens of relevant publications monthly, creating what feels like an insurmountable information burden.

Tools that may be beneficial for synthesizing and summarizing literature include Semantic Scholar, Scholarcy, and Notebook LM. Semantic Scholar functions as a publication research tool that quickly identifies manuscripts of interest that have PDFs for easy access and is sortable by recency and most influential work. After identifying a paper of interest you may want to read or present, Scholarcy can quickly summarize the work and export key summaries and findings to Word or PowerPoint.

Notebook LM from Google provides an incredible solution for MSLs who are continuously traveling and may not be able to sit down and thumb through a paper or read a screen. With input from a website URL, a PDF, or written text, Notebook LM outputs a conversational podcast with a naturally flowing discussion of key details and findings of a study. For individuals who have varying learning approaches, Notebook LM gives an alternative learning option for MSLs on the go.

While the outputs from these tools are imperfect, they can expedite your research and preparation for a journal club.

Open Evidence is another incredible emerging resource for providers and medical affairs professionals. It is currently being utilized by 40% of healthcare providers (HCPs) on a daily bases with approximately 65,000 new verified U.S. clinician registrants every month. This tool is free for verified U.S. HCPs, is practical, and can be used as to create point-of-care tools such as helping draft clinical notes.

While these tools can provide wonderful summaries and drastically cut down on time, you must always be vigilant for pesky hallucinations, or fabricated information that seem plausible but are not based in fact.

Scientific Narrative Development

Modern MSLs must craft compelling narratives from complex scientific data. Publications represent an individual data point that tells part of a story. Through leveraging a large language model (LLM) like ChatGPT or Claude, you can create an effective scientific narrative that integrates these individual data points into a compelling story. This is where having a deep understanding of your KOLs and the care barriers that are specific to your territory becomes critical. This deep understanding will enable you to improve your prompt for the LLM to craft individualized narratives that are specific to each of your individual KOL's needs.

An example prompt might look like this: Create a brief scientific narrative for Dr. Sarah Mitchell, a rural family medicine physician in Mississippi who specializes in hypertension management and has published research on medication adherence barriers in underserved populations. Base the narrative on this recent publication: "Community Health Worker-Led Hypertension Control in Rural Settings: Results from the RURAL-BP Randomized Trial" published in *JAMA Internal Medicine*, March 2024, which showed that community health worker interventions achieved 15.2 mmHg greater systolic BP reduction compared to usual care in rural communities, with particular benefit in African American patients (18.1 mmHg reduction). The study enrolled 847 patients across 12 rural counties in the Southeast.

The output might look like this: Dr. Mitchell, the recent RURAL-BP trial published *in JAMA Internal Medicine* provides compelling validation for the community-based interventions you've championed in your Mississippi practice. The study's finding of a 15.2 mmHg systolic blood pressure reduction through community health worker (CHW) interventions directly supports your published work on addressing medication adherence barriers in underserved populations. Most significantly for your patient demographics, the trial demonstrated an 18.1 mmHg reduction in African American participants—a population that comprises a substantial portion of rural Southern communities and faces disproportionate hypertension burden.

The 847-patient trial across 12 rural Southeastern counties mirrors the challenges you encounter daily: limited specialist access, transportation barriers, and complex socioeconomic factors affecting medication adherence. The CHW model's success in achieving blood pressure control rates of 72% versus 48% in usual care validates your advocacy for task-shifting strategies and community engagement approaches. These findings strengthen the evidence base for scaling CHW programs as a practical solution to the rural hypertension crisis you've documented, offering health systems a proven intervention that addresses both clinical outcomes and health equity simultaneously.

The devil is in a detailed prompt to have an effective message. This example highlights the capability of an LLM to have personalized focus based on the clinician's background, setting, research interests, and patient population. This will make data resonate with the KOL and strengthen your bond because of your care for their individual needs.

KOL Engagement and Relationship Management

Another effective use of LLMs is through the preparation of discussion guides for group meetings or through the creation of topics and questions for an advisory board that are regionally specific.

An example prompt might look like this: Create an outline for a discussion guide for a multidisciplinary team meeting between primary care physicians, endocrinologists, and heart failure cardiologists discussing optimal GLP-1 receptor agonist use in patients with obesity and comorbid heart failure. Include decision points for therapy initiation, monitoring parameters, and care coordination responsibilities. Focus on practical clinical scenarios and evidence-based recommendations.

The output could provide recommendations on pre-call planning integrating critical topics like guideline-directed medical therapy, dosing strategies, timing strategies in relation to other interventions, monitoring protocols, and a multidisciplinary care communication framework. You can further refine your prompt to create questions to drive conversation on specific topics that will elicit insights that are critical to your medical strategy.

AI-Driven Analysis of Field Medical Intelligence

Bringing in insights from the field is one of the most crucial components of the MSL role. Much of the time these insights feel like they get lost in a black hole on the backend of customer relationship management software. That's because this is intensive work to painstakingly read through the tens or hundreds of individual insights that are pulled in by the field medical team before formulating what they mean and determining what actions you might want to take. As an MSL insights lead, you can expedite this process by feeding the raw data into an LLM, sift through the noise, and isolate the signal to inform your medical strategy and communications.

An example prompt might look like this: Analyze the following input and create a structured summary organized around four key themes: (1) Diagnostic barriers and challenges in disease identification, (2) Solutions to overcome care delivery barriers, (3) Key differentiators between available therapies, and (4) Clinical or technological innovations. For each theme, extract relevant information from the input, provide specific examples or data points when available, and maintain focus on actionable insights. If any theme is not addressed in the source material, note this explicitly. Limit the summary to specify length: e.g., 300 words, 2 pages.

With respect to insight summaries, these AI models aren't trained to recognize the most critical information for your specific medical strategy. An insight reported by eight community physicians may carry far less strategic weight than a single observation from a national thought leader whose research shapes clinical guidelines. AI excels at aggregating volume but struggles with nuance—it cannot assess whether feedback comes from early adopters or late-stage skeptics, whether concerns reflect genuine clinical barriers or reimbursement frustrations, or whether enthusiasm signals true practice-changing potential or simply academic interest. The algorithm doesn't know that Dr. Smith chairs the committee revising treatment guidelines, that the safety question from Dr. Johnson mirrors concerns the FDA raised in your last advisory meeting, or that the efficacy gap mentioned by Dr. Lee represents your product's key differentiator from the competitor launching next quarter.

Remember, the power is in the prompt. When crafting your prompts, here are some do's and don'ts.

DO'S

1. **Be hyperspecific about your audience:** Include KOL's specialty, geographic location, research interests, and patient demographics. "Rural family physician in Texas treating predominantly Hispanic diabetic population" generates far better content than "physician."
2. **Anchor everything in real evidence:** Always reference specific publications with journal names, dates, and concrete data points. "Based on the CANVAS trial (*NEJM* 2017) showing 14% cardiovascular risk reduction" creates credible, citable content.
3. **Set clear format and length boundaries:** Specify exactly what you want: "2-paragraph email," "5-bullet summary," or "200-word narrative." LLMs need structure to deliver usable outputs.
4. **Create personal connection points:** Link new evidence to the KOL's published work or known clinical interests. "This validates your 2022 research on medication adherence in rural populations."
5. **Include practical clinical context:** Specify relevant considerations like drug interactions, patient compliance issues, insurance coverage, or practice workflow integration that affect real-world implementation.

DON'TS

1. **Don't use vague, generic prompts:** Avoid requests like "create content about diabetes." These generate textbook-level information that provides no unique value to sophisticated medical professionals.
2. **Don't forget regulatory compliance context:** Always specify "ensure compliance with promotional guidelines" and "include appropriate medical disclaimers" to avoid generating problematic content.
3. **Don't overwhelm with multiple requests:** Asking for "an email template, discussion guide, and manuscript summary" in one prompt dilutes focus. Make separate, targeted requests for better results.
4. **Don't skip the evidence foundation:** Content without specific research citations appears unprofessional and unsubstantiated to medical audiences who expect evidence-based information.
5. **Don't neglect iterative refinement:** Your first prompt output is a starting point, not a final product. Use follow-up prompts like "make this more technical for cardiologists" or "add specific dosing recommendations" to optimize results.

OpenEvidence: Transforming Clinical Information Access and MSL Engagement

On the provider side, OpenEvidence represents a paradigm shift in how clinicians access and process medical information, emerging as the fastest-adopted clinical tool in healthcare history. Used by over 40% of U.S. physicians across more than 10,000 hospitals and medical centers, the AI-powered platform allows clinicians to ask natural language questions and receive immediate, evidence-based answers grounded in peer-reviewed research from sources like *NEJM* and *JAMA*. With over 8.5 million monthly clinical consultations and growth of 65,000 new physician registrations each month, OpenEvidence has fundamentally altered the information landscape that MSLs must navigate. Clinical uses for providers include asking clinical questions, assisting with patient workups, evaluating treatment options, identifying evidence, consulting guidelines, and even functionally writing prior authorization letters or insurance appeals or write a patient handout.

For MSLs, OpenEvidence represents both an opportunity and a strategic imperative. The platform provides accurate, evidence-based recommendations that align with physician treatment plans sourcing exclusively from millions of peer-reviewed publications. MSLs must understand how these data inform their target clinicians' decision-making. Rather than competing with this technology, successful MSLs can leverage OpenEvidence as a complementary tool to enhance their scientific discussions and use it as a gateway for pipeline discussions and lean into strategic relationship building. The platform's HIPAA compliance and integration into clinical workflows means it has become part of the decision-making infrastructure that MSLs must understand to remain relevant.

The emergence of OpenEvidence signals a broader transformation in how scientific influence operates in healthcare. As more than 100 million Americans are now treated by physicians using the platform. MSLs who adapt their engagement strategies to complement AI-driven information access will maintain their competitive advantage. This requires shifting from being primary information providers to becoming strategic interpreters and contextualizers of evidence—helping clinicians understand not just what the data says, but how it applies to specific patient populations and clinical scenarios. The most effective MSLs will use tools like OpenEvidence to elevate their conversations from basic information transfer to sophisticated scientific dialogue that adds genuine value to clinical decision-making.

THE HUMAN–AI PARTNERSHIP AND QUALITY CONTROL

While AI can process information faster than humans, it cannot replace scientific judgment. Every AI-generated insight must be validated against your expertise and understanding of the therapeutic area. The most effective AI implementation follows systematic best practices: always fact-check AI-generated summaries against original sources, maintain awareness of AI limitations and potential biases, use AI as a starting point rather than an endpoint for analysis, and develop consistent approaches for reviewing AI outputs. This critical evaluation ensures that efficiency gains do not come at the expense of scientific rigor or accuracy. MSLs must remember that AI tools can hallucinate information, misinterpret complex clinical concepts, or fail to understand nuanced regulatory requirements that are second nature to experienced medical professionals.

REGULATORY AND COMPLIANCE FRAMEWORK

The pharmaceutical industry operates under strict regulatory guidelines that must be respected when using AI tools. Data privacy represents a fundamental concern—all AI platforms must comply with HIPAA, GDPR, and other relevant regulations, particularly when processing patient information or proprietary clinical data. AI-generated content must meet industry standards for scientific accuracy and fair balance, requiring careful review to ensure promotional guidelines are followed. Organizations should maintain comprehensive documentation of AI tool usage for audit purposes and establish formal validation processes for AI-generated insights before sharing with stakeholders. This includes creating clear protocols for reviewing AI outputs, defining approval workflows for AI-assisted communications, and training teams on both the capabilities and limitations of these technologies. The goal is to harness AI's efficiency while maintaining the compliance standards and scientific integrity that define responsible medical affairs practice. It's critical to be aware of company restrictions and never uploading proprietary confidential information into a third-party AI agent to ensure you're not violating company rules.

CONCLUSION: AI AS AN AMPLIFIER OF MSL EXCELLENCE

AI represents a transformative tool for MSLs, but its true value lies not in replacing human expertise, but in amplifying the uniquely human capabilities that drive success in medical affairs. AI can rapidly synthesize literature, generate scientific narratives, create discussion guides, and collate actionable insights from complex datasets—tasks that traditionally consumed hours of an MSL's day. However, these technological capabilities only become meaningful when combined with the critical thinking, relationship-building skills, and scientific judgment that define exceptional MSL performance. The technology handles the information processing; the MSL provides the strategic insight, clinical context, and stakeholder understanding that transforms raw data into compelling scientific communications.

Simon Sinek's observation that "In the future, the skills that machines can't replace, our care, our reason, and our humanity, will be the keys to success" captures the essence of AI's role in medical affairs. While AI can draft a scientific narrative based on clinical trial data, it cannot understand the personal research interests of a KOL, navigate the complex dynamics of a medical advisory board, or provide the empathetic counsel that builds lasting professional relationships. The MSL's ability to synthesize not just scientific evidence but also human motivations, institutional politics, and individual clinical experiences remains irreplaceable. AI enhances these soft skills by removing routine tasks, allowing MSLs to focus on high-value activities like strategic thinking, relationship cultivation, and complex problem-solving that require human insight and emotional intelligence.

The integration of AI into MSL workflows is no longer optional—it is becoming a competitive necessity. Organizations are increasingly seeking professionals who can leverage these tools effectively while maintaining the scientific rigor and interpersonal skills that drive medical affairs success. MSLs should actively experiment with AI platforms, become proficient in prompt engineering techniques, and develop a nuanced understanding of both the capabilities and limitations of these technologies. The accompanying "AI Learning Guide for Medical Affairs Professionals" in *Workaid* provides a roadmap for adopting AI into your workflows and advancement to an AI champion.

This hands-on experience not only improves daily productivity but also positions MSLs as valuable internal resources who can educate colleagues, guide organizational AI adoption strategies, and speak knowledgeably about these tools during interviews. The future belongs to MSLs who can seamlessly blend AI with authentic human connection, using technology to amplify their scientific expertise while remaining fundamentally grounded in the care, reason, and humanity that make medical affairs meaningful.

CHAPTER 5 TAKEAWAYS: THE AI REVOLUTION IN MEDICAL AFFAIRS

Strategic AI Integration

- Have you identified specific AI applications that enhance your daily MSL workflow without compromising strategic focus?
- Can you demonstrate how AI amplifies your human expertise rather than replacing your core competencies?
- Do you understand the competitive advantage AI proficiency provides in medical affairs career advancement?
- Can you articulate how AI amplifies human expertise rather than replace core MSL competencies during interviews and career discussions?

Literature Management and Scientific Communication

- Have you mastered tools like Semantic Scholar, Scholarcy, and Notebook LM for efficient literature monitoring and synthesis?
- Can you articulate the impact of OpenEvidence and your plan to evolve with emerging tools?
- Can you create personalized scientific narratives using LLMs that resonate with individual KOL backgrounds and interests?
- Are you able to transform complex scientific data into compelling, audience-specific communications?

Quality Control and Compliance

- Have you established systematic processes for fact-checking AI-generated content and maintaining awareness of regulatory requirements (HIPAA, GDPR, promotional guidelines)?
- Can you maintain the critical balance between AI efficiency and scientific rigor, using technology as a starting point rather than an endpoint for analysis?

The Science of Influence 6

Finding Your Path Forward

"You now possess the blueprint. The question isn't whether you have what it takes—it's whether you'll apply what you've learned with the persistence and authenticity that transforms aspiration into achievement. This is your calling, your opportunity, and your science of influence."

John's story of coordinated care at the beginning of the book illustrates the profound impact Medical Science Liaisons (MSLs) create through strategic relationship building and evidence-based education. The surgeon who recognized amyloid deposits, the neurologist who pursued genetic testing, the cardiologist who established monitoring protocols—each played their role, but the MSL's behind-the-scenes influence created the conditions that made this excellence possible. This is the essence of influence in medical affairs: creating change not through direct intervention, but through strategic positioning that amplifies impact exponentially.

THE FOUNDATION: CORE MSL EXCELLENCE

An MSL's success rests on integrated competencies that define exceptional performance across all therapeutic areas and career stages. The CEO mindset transforms you from individual contributor to strategic orchestrator of complex stakeholder ecosystems, viewing every relationship as an opportunity for mutual value creation. Authentic relationship building becomes your

DOI: 10.1201/9781003781547-6

competitive advantage, distinguishing transactional interactions from genuine professional partnerships built on mutual respect and consistent follow-through. Scientific excellence provides the non-negotiable foundation—demanding deep understanding of methodologies, competitive landscapes, and real-world applications while requiring intellectual humility to acknowledge knowledge limitations. Strategic insight generation elevates your role from information provider to organizational asset, translating field observations into actionable intelligence that informs clinical development, competitive positioning, and market strategy.

These competencies operate synergistically rather than independently. Your scientific credibility enables access to influential stakeholders, authentic relationships provide platforms for meaningful education, strategic insights demonstrate organizational value, and the CEO mindset integrates everything into coherent territory management that creates sustainable impact.

ANTICIPATION OF TOMORROW'S MEDICAL AFFAIRS

The MSL role continues evolving rapidly, driven by scientific complexity, regulatory changes, and technological innovation that reshape how medical information is created and disseminated. Success requires adaptive capabilities that enable thriving amid ongoing change while maintaining the fundamental relationship-building skills that define MSL value.

Artificial intelligence integration represents the most significant immediate evolution, offering unprecedented opportunities to amplify human expertise rather than replace it. AI enables MSLs to process information more efficiently while focusing their unique capabilities on relationship building, strategic thinking, and complex problem-solving requiring emotional intelligence. Your AI proficiency becomes a career differentiator, positioning you for advancement opportunities while demonstrating innovation leadership that guides organizational transformation.

Simultaneously, stakeholder expectations continue elevating. Healthcare providers increasingly expect MSLs to function as strategic partners understanding health economics, real-world evidence, and implementation challenges affecting patient care delivery. Internal stakeholders expect insights informing clinical development strategies and commercial positioning rather than simply executing predefined activities. This evolution creates opportunities for greater impact and career advancement while demanding higher-level analytical thinking and business acumen.

CREATING YOUR PROFESSIONAL LEGACY

Building a distinctive professional brand that highlights your unique value proposition becomes essential as competition intensifies. This involves developing thought leadership through combining therapeutic area expertise with unique perspectives on clinical challenges, investing in professional networks through mutual value creation rather than one-sided relationship building, and committing to lifelong learning extending beyond immediate role requirements.

Your influence creates ripple effects throughout healthcare ecosystems benefiting patients you may never meet. Every successful scientific exchange influences treatment decisions for hundreds of future patients. Every barrier you help remove improves outcomes for entire populations. Every collaboration you facilitate between specialists creates care pathways with generational impact. The cumulative effect of these activities creates a legacy of improved patient care extending far beyond individual achievements, providing the motivation that sustains MSL careers while creating deep satisfaction from meaningful work aligned with personal values.

THE PATH FORWARD

Success requires developing a clear vision for your career trajectory encompassing long-term objectives for therapeutic expertise, leadership development, and professional impact. Balance ambitious professional goals with authentic personal values for sustainable career satisfaction. Invest systematically in relationship maintenance through consistent value creation and meaningful engagement. Embrace continuous innovation by seeking opportunities to improve effectiveness and expand impact. Develop systems for tracking and communicating your impact, translating activities into business outcomes and patient benefit stories that resonate with diverse audiences.

YOUR SCIENCE OF INFLUENCE

John's coordinated care experience resulted from an MSL's persistent work to educate stakeholders, facilitate collaborations, and remove obstacles preventing optimal care delivery. This represents your opportunity and responsibility: to work behind the scenes ensuring scientific advances translate into clinical practice improvements that transform patient lives.

Whether you're preparing for your first MSL interview or seeking career advancement, the strategies in this book provide your roadmap to success. The self-assessment frameworks help you articulate your authentic passion and unique value proposition with conviction. The networking approaches transform you from an anonymous applicant to a known candidate with internal advocates. The interview preparation techniques position you to demonstrate readiness rather than just qualification. The AI integration strategies differentiate you as an innovative professional prepared for tomorrow's medical affairs landscape.

But knowledge without action creates no change. The MSL role demands persistent execution of relationship building, scientific communication, and strategic thinking over months and years. The candidates who succeed are those who implement these strategies consistently, learn from setbacks, and maintain unwavering commitment to breaking into this competitive field. Your transition into medical affairs requires not just understanding these concepts, but living them through every networking conversation, every customized application, and every interview interaction.

The skills you develop through this process—strategic thinking, authentic relationship building, scientific communication, and systematic barrier removal—position you to create profound healthcare impact while building a personally fulfilling career. Your commitment to excellence contributes not just to personal success, but to advancing medical affairs as a strategic discipline creating meaningful patient care impact.

MSLs who understand that influence emerges not from authority, but from authentic expertise, genuine relationships, and unwavering commitment to advancing the science that improves human health separate themselves from the field. You now possess the blueprint. The question isn't whether you have what it takes—it's whether you'll apply what you've learned with the persistence and authenticity that transforms aspiration into achievement. This is your calling, your opportunity, and your science of influence.

MSL Job Networking Workaid

Note: Please use this workaid as a guide, not as doctrine.

PHASE ONE: SETUP AND PREPARATION

LinkedIn Optimization Checklist

- [ ] LinkedIn Premium subscription secured
- [ ] Profile optimized with MSL keywords
- [ ] Professional headshot updated
- [ ] 500+ pharma/biotech connections

Target Role Documentation

- **Company:** ________________________ **Position:** ______________ ____________________
- **Therapeutic Area:** ________________________ **Deadline:** ______ ____________________

PHASE TWO: STAKEHOLDER IDENTIFICATION

Key Players to Research

ROLE	NAME	LINKEDIN PROFILE	CONTACT INFO
Current MSL #1			
Current MSL #2			
Recruiter			
Hiring Manager			

Research Strategies

- Company website team pages
- LinkedIn company employee search
- Professional networks leveraged

PHASE THREE: MSL INFORMATIONAL INTERVIEW

Initial Outreach Template

Subject: Seeking insights about MSL opportunities at [Company]

"Hi [MSL Name], I'm exploring MSL opportunities and came across the [Position Title] role at [Company]. Would you be open to a brief 15–20 minute conversation to share insights about your experience with the team? I'd greatly appreciate learning from your expertise. Best regards, [Your Name]"

Strategic Question Bank *(Be Curious First, Salesperson Second)*

Role and Territory: Can you tell me about your territory size and travel requirements? What does a typical week look like?

Team and Culture: How would you describe the team dynamics? What's the makeup of your MSL team? How do you interact with the hiring manager?

Challenges and Solutions: What are the biggest challenges you face? How have you worked to overcome these? What skills are most important for success?

Performance and Growth: How are MSLs evaluated? What advancement opportunities exist? How does the company support development?

Company Direction: Do you enjoy working for [Company]? Where is the company heading? How has it evolved since you joined?

30-Second Elevator Pitch Framework

"I'm a [Your Background] with [X years] of experience in [Relevant Area]. I'm interested in this role because [Reason 1: Specific to Company], [Reason 2: Your Unique Value], and [Reason 3: Your Motivation]. My background in [Specific Experience] would enable me to [Value You'd Bring]."
Your Pitch: ____

____

Conversation Flow Strategy

Opening (2–3 min): Thank them, brief intro, explain interest
Information Gathering (10–15 min): Ask prepared questions, listen actively, take notes
Your Background (3–5 min): Wait for them to ask, deliver 30-second pitch, provide 2–3 specific reasons
Closing (2–3 min): Express appreciation, ask about resume review, request internal referral

---

PHASE FOUR: POST-INTERVIEW ACTION

Immediate Follow-up (Within 24 hours)

- Thank you message sent
- Resume shared (if agreed)
- Internal referral requested
- LinkedIn connection maintained

Thank You Template

"Hi [MSL Name], Thank you for speaking with me about the MSL role. Your insights about [Specific Topic] were invaluable and increased my enthusiasm for the position. As discussed, I've attached my resume. If comfortable, I would appreciate an internal referral for the [Position Title] role. Thank you again. Best regards, [Your Name]"

PHASE FIVE: RECRUITER AND HIRING MANAGER OUTREACH

Recruiter Contact Template

"Hi [Recruiter Name], I'm writing regarding the [Position Title] role. I've had a positive conversation with [MSL Name] and applied with an internal referral. I'd welcome discussing how my background in [Experience] aligns with your needs. Available for a brief conversation this week? Best regards, [Your Name]"

Hiring Manager Contact Template

"Hi [Manager Name], I'm very interested in the [Position Title] opportunity and had an excellent conversation with [MSL Name] about your team. I've applied with an internal referral and would appreciate discussing how my experience could contribute to your objectives. Available for a brief conversation? Best regards, [Your Name]"

PHASE SIX: COMMUNICATION EXCELLENCE

Interaction Standards *(Every Communication Is Part of Your Interview)*

- Professional tone maintained
- Grammar and spelling checked
- Prompt response (within 24 hours)
- Complete information included
- Respectful of their time
- Genuine appreciation expressed

Critical Success Factors

- Be genuinely curious about their experience
- Listen more than you speak
- Ask thoughtful follow-up questions
- Show genuine appreciation
- Be easy to talk to and likeable
- Maintain professionalism throughout
- Follow through on all commitments

PHASE SEVEN: TRACKING AND RESULTS

Progress Tracking

Contact	Role	Initial Contact	Meeting Complete	Referral Status

Success Metrics

- **MSL Conversations Completed: [ ]**
- **Internal Referrals Secured: [ ]**
- **Recruiter Responses: [ ]**
- **Interview Invitations: [ ]**

Red Flags to Avoid

- Don't oversell yourself initially
- Don't dominate conversations
- Don't ask for referrals too early
- Don't forget to follow up
- Don't be pushy or aggressive

Long-term Relationship Building

- Stay connected on LinkedIn
- Share relevant industry articles occasionally
- Update them on job search progress
- Thank them when you land a role
- Offer to help others in their network

QUICK REFERENCE REMINDERS

Key Insight: Internal referral bonuses often exceed $1,000, making current employees motivated to help qualified candidates.

Success Formula: Professional engagement + Genuine curiosity + Strategic follow-up = Internal referral = Interview opportunity

Timeline: Initial contact → Response (5–7 days) → Meeting (within 2 weeks) → Follow-up (24 hours) → Referral request → Recruiter/Manager outreach

Final Note: Your goal is to demonstrate that you're worth the referral investment through professional, thoughtful engagement that shows you understand the role and would be a valuable team member.

QUESTION BANK FOR MSL INTERVIEWS

QUESTIONS FOR HR REPRESENTATIVES

Territory and Role Logistics

- "Can you describe the geographic territory and typical travel expectations for this role?"
- "How does the company support MSLs in managing travel demands while maintaining work-life balance?"

- "What does a typical MSL schedule look like in terms of weekly travel patterns?"
- "Are there any upcoming changes to territory boundaries or coverage areas?"
- "How flexible is the travel schedule, and what notice is typically given for conference attendance?"

Team Structure and Composition

- "What is the current size and composition of the MSL team?"
- "How many MSLs will I be working alongside in this therapeutic area?"
- "What backgrounds do current team members have (PhD, PharmD, MD, clinical experience)?"
- "How does the MSL team collaborate with other medical affairs functions?"
- "Is this a new position or a replacement for someone who left?"

Professional Development and Growth

- "What professional development opportunities does the company provide for medical affairs professionals?"
- "How does the company support MSLs in staying current with scientific developments?"
- "Are there opportunities for conference attendance and presentation?"
- "What does career progression typically look like within medical affairs?"
- "Does the company provide funding for additional certifications or training programs?"

Performance and Evaluation

- "How do you typically measure MSL success and effectiveness?"
- "What does the performance evaluation process look like?"
- "How frequently are performance reviews conducted?"
- "What metrics are most important for MSL performance assessment?"

Company Culture and Resources

- "How would you describe the company culture, particularly within medical affairs?"
- "What resources and tools does the company provide to support MSL effectiveness?"
- "How does the company foster collaboration between different departments?"
- "What makes this company an attractive place to build a medical affairs career?"

QUESTIONS FOR HIRING MANAGERS

Role Expectations and Success Metrics

- "How will you measure my success in this role during the first 30 days, 90 days, and first year?"
- "What does excellence look like for MSLs on your team?"
- "What would you expect me to accomplish in my first six months?"
- "How do you define success for this specific territory or therapeutic area?"
- "What are the most important KPIs for MSLs in your organization?"

Strategic Direction and Vision

- "What are you most excited about regarding the company's direction and the medical affairs team's role in that growth?"
- "What opportunities do you see emerging in this therapeutic area over the next 2–3 years?"
- "How does medical affairs contribute to the company's overall strategic objectives?"
- "What role do MSLs play in supporting product lifecycle management?"
- "How do you see the MSL role evolving within your organization?"

Team Culture and Management Style

- "From a cultural and collaborative standpoint, what characteristics define your most successful team members?"
- "How do you prefer to work with and support your MSLs?"
- "What is your management and communication style?"
- "How do you handle situations when team members face challenges or setbacks?"
- "What does collaboration look like between MSLs and other medical affairs functions?"

Challenges and Opportunities

- "What are the biggest challenges and opportunities facing the medical affairs team currently?"
- "How would this role contribute to addressing those strategic priorities?"
- "What obstacles do MSLs in this therapeutic area typically encounter?"
- "What competitive challenges exist in this market, and how does medical affairs address them?"
- "What keeps you up at night regarding this therapeutic area or market?"

Development and Growth

- "How does the medical affairs organization support career development and advancement?"
- "What growth opportunities exist for high-performing MSLs?"
- "How do you help team members develop new skills and capabilities?"
- "What mentoring or coaching do you provide to your team members?"
- "How do you support MSLs who want to transition to different roles within medical affairs?"

Ideal Candidate Profile

- "What qualities distinguish your most successful MSLs from good performers?"

- "What would make someone particularly successful in this specific role?"
- "What characteristics or experiences would help someone excel in this territory?"
- "What skills or competencies are you most hoping to add to your team?"
- "What type of candidate would complement the existing team dynamics?"

QUESTIONS FOR CURRENT MSL TEAM MEMBERS

Day-to-Day Role Reality

- "What does a typical week look like for you in this role?"
- "What aspects of the MSL work do you find most rewarding and most challenging?"
- "How much time do you spend on different activities like travel, meetings, administrative work?"
- "What surprised you most about the role when you first started?"
- "How has your role evolved since you joined the company?"

Professional Growth and Development

- "How has your own career developed since joining this team?"
- "What learning opportunities have been most valuable for your development?"
- "What skills have you developed that you didn't expect to need?"
- "How does the company support your professional growth and advancement?"
- "What advice would you give to someone just starting as an MSL?"

Team Dynamics and Collaboration

- "How would you describe the collaborative culture within the medical affairs team?"
- "How do team members support each other's success?"

- "What does communication and coordination look like among MSLs?"
- "How often do you interact with your fellow MSLs?"
- "What makes this team special or unique compared to other places you've worked?"

Work-Life Integration

- "How do you manage the travel requirements and maintain personal relationships and interests?"
- "What strategies have you developed for managing work-life balance?"
- "How flexible is the schedule for personal commitments and family obligations?"
- "What does the company do to support employee well-being?"
- "How do you handle the isolation that can come with field-based work?"

Stakeholder Relationships

- "What types of healthcare providers do you work with most frequently?"
- "What makes a KOL interaction successful from your perspective?"
- "What barriers or challenges do you currently experience with stakeholders?"
- "How have you built strong relationships with key opinion leaders?"
- "What do you wish healthcare providers better understood about the MSL role?"

Company and Therapeutic Area Perspective

- "What developments in this therapeutic area or within the company are you most excited about?"
- "How would you describe the competitive landscape in this market?"
- "What makes this company different from other pharmaceutical organizations?"
- "What do you see as the biggest opportunities in this therapeutic area?"
- "If you could change one thing about your role or the company, what would it be?"

Future Outlook

- "Where do you see your career heading within medical affairs?"
- "What trends do you see shaping the MSL role in the coming years?"
- "How do you think this therapeutic area will evolve?"
- "What skills do you think will become more important for future MSL success?"

QUESTIONS FOR PANEL INTERVIEW/ PRESENTATION

Strategic Thinking

- "How does this therapeutic area fit into the company's broader strategic portfolio and treatment landscape?"
- "What role do you see MSLs playing in advancing awareness of [Therapeutic Area/Condition] within your organization's strategy?"
- "How does the team prioritize which healthcare providers and stakeholders to engage with new scientific information?"
- "What barriers has the team encountered when trying to implement new scientific findings in clinical practice?"
- "How does the organization measure the impact and effectiveness of MSL scientific engagement with stakeholders?"

COLLABORATION AND CROSS-FUNCTIONAL WORK

- "How do MSLs collaborate with commercial colleagues to ensure appropriate scientific communication boundaries?"
- "What role do MSLs typically play in advisory board discussions and medical education programs within this organization?"
- "How do MSLs collaborate with medical information and publications teams on emerging scientific topics?"
- "What types of insights from field interactions are most valuable to share with internal medical affairs colleagues?"

PROBLEM-SOLVING AND ADAPTATION

- "How does the team typically handle situations where healthcare providers challenge research conclusions or company data?"
- "What approach do you recommend when stakeholders have conflicting interpretations of clinical data?"
- "What resources or escalation processes are available when MSLs encounter questions they can't answer during KOL interactions?"
- "What strategies have been most effective when engaging with skeptical or disengaged healthcare providers?"

PROFESSIONAL DEVELOPMENT

- "What aspects of this scientific area should new MSLs prioritize learning to better support healthcare providers?"
- "How does the organization support MSLs in staying current with evolving research in this therapeutic area?"
- "What additional expertise or resources does the company provide to enhance MSL effectiveness in scientific discussions?"

FINAL QUESTIONS

- "What questions do you have about my background or experience that would help you assess my fit for this role?"
- "Is there anything about my qualifications or approach that you'd like me to clarify or expand upon?"
- "What would you expect me to accomplish in my first 90 days, and how would you measure early success?"
- "What additional information can you provide to help me determine if this opportunity aligns with my career goals?"

QUESTION SELECTION STRATEGY

Prioritization Guidelines

- **Choose 3–5 questions maximum per stakeholder** to avoid overwhelming the conversation. You may only have time for 1 or 2.
- **Select questions that demonstrate your research and preparation** about the company and role
- **Focus on questions that help you make an informed decision** about the opportunity
- **Avoid questions easily answered by public information** (company website, job posting)
- **Prepare follow-up questions** based on their responses to show active listening

Customization Tips

- **Adapt questions based on the conversation flow** and information already shared
- **Reference specific company initiatives or recent developments** when appropriate
- **Connect your questions to your background and interests** to show authentic engagement
- **Use their responses to ask deeper follow-up questions** that demonstrate strategic thinking

Remember: The questions you ask are as important as the answers you give—they demonstrate your preparation, strategic thinking, and genuine interest in the role and organization.

MSL BEHAVIORAL INTERVIEW QUESTIONS AND STAR RESPONSE WORKSHEET

This comprehensive workaid provides interviewing MSLs with 25 real-world behavioral interview questions and a structured STAR method worksheet to develop compelling, professional responses. Rather than attempting to memorize answers for every possible question, this strategic approach helps you identify 8–10 versatile professional anecdotes that can be adapted to address multiple behavioral scenarios while demonstrating the key competencies hiring managers seek in medical affairs professionals. Use this resource to transform your authentic experiences into polished interview responses that showcase your readiness for MSL success.

25 COMMON MSL BEHAVIORAL INTERVIEW QUESTIONS

Leadership and Influence

1. "Tell me about a time when you had to influence others without formal authority to achieve a goal."
2. "Describe a situation where you had to lead a team or project with competing priorities or resistant stakeholders."
3. "Give me an example of when you mentored or coached someone. What was your approach and what was the outcome?"

Communication and Presentation

4. "Tell me about a time when you had to present complex scientific information to an audience with varying levels of expertise. How did you approach this challenge?"
5. "Describe a situation where you had to adapt your communication style for a difficult or unresponsive audience."
6. "Give me an example of when you had to deliver bad news or disappointing results to stakeholders. How did you handle it?"
7. "Tell me about a time when you had to explain a controversial or unpopular decision to colleagues or stakeholders."

Relationship Building and Stakeholder Management

8. "Describe a time when you had to build a relationship with a challenging or skeptical stakeholder. What was your strategy?"

9. "Tell me about a situation where you had to manage multiple competing stakeholders with different agendas."
10. "Give me an example of when you turned a negative relationship into a positive one. What steps did you take?"
11. "Describe a time when you had to work with someone whose working style was very different from yours."

Problem-Solving and Innovation

12. "Tell me about a complex problem you solved when the solution wasn't immediately obvious. Walk me through your thought process."
13. "Describe a time when you identified an opportunity that others had missed. How did you approach it?"
14. "Give me an example of when you had to find a creative solution with limited resources or constraints."
15. "Tell me about a time when you had to troubleshoot a process or system that wasn't working effectively."

Adaptability and Resilience

16. "Describe a time when you had to quickly adapt to significant changes in your work environment, priorities, or responsibilities."
17. "Tell me about a professional setback or failure you experienced. How did you handle it and what did you learn?"
18. "Give me an example of when you had to work under pressure or tight deadlines. How did you manage the situation?"
19. "Describe a time when you received critical feedback. How did you respond and what actions did you take?"

Learning and Development

20. "Tell me about a time when you had to quickly master a new skill, technology, or knowledge area for your work."
21. "Describe a situation where you realized you made a mistake. How did you handle it and what did you learn?"
22. "Give me an example of when you had to research and become an expert on a topic outside your normal area of expertise."

Collaboration and Teamwork

23. "Tell me about a time when you had to resolve a conflict or disagreement within a team. What was your approach?"
24. "Describe a situation where you had to coordinate efforts across multiple departments or functions to achieve a goal."
25. "Give me an example of when you had to give honest feedback to a peer or colleague about their performance or approach."

STAR METHOD RESPONSE WORKSHEET

STAR Framework Overview

- **S**ituation: Set the context and background
- **T**ask: Explain your specific role and responsibilities
- **A**ction: Describe the specific actions you took
- **R**esult: Share the outcomes and lessons learned

RESPONSE DEVELOPMENT WORKSHEET

Question Being Addressed:

Write the specific behavioral question you're preparing to answer:

____

____

Situation (Context and Background)

Provide clear, concise context about the challenge or opportunity. Include relevant details about timeline, location, people involved, and circumstances.

When did this occur? ________________________________

____

Where did this take place? ______________________________

____

Who was involved? ______________________________

____

What was the general context/background? ____________________

____

____

____

____

____

What made this situation challenging or significant? ____________

____

____

____

____

____

Task (Your Role and Responsibilities)

Explain your specific role and what you were responsible for achieving.

What was your specific role in this situation? ____________________

____

____

____

What were you trying to accomplish? ______________________

____

____

____

What constraints or challenges did you face? ____________________

____

____

____

What was at stake if you didn't succeed? ______________________

____

____

____

Action (Specific Steps You Took)

Describe the specific actions you took. Focus on YOUR contributions, not what the team did.

What was your first step? ____________________________________

____

____

____

What specific actions did you take to address the challenge? ________

____

____

____

____

____

____

____

How did you involve or work with others? _______________________

____

____

What resources did you use or seek out? ____________________

____

____

____

How did you handle obstacles or resistance? ____________________

____

____

____

What was your decision-making process? ____________________

____

____

____

Result (Outcomes and Learning)

Share the outcomes achieved and lessons learned from the experience.

What was the immediate outcome? ____________________

____

____

____

What were the longer-term results or impact? ____________________

____

____

____

How did you measure success? ____________________

____

____

____

What positive feedback did you receive? ___________________________

____

____

____

What did you learn from this experience? ___________________________

____

____

____

How did this experience change your approach to similar situations?

____

____

____

How is this relevant to the MSL role you're applying for? __________

____

____

____

____

____

____

____

RESPONSE REFINEMENT CHECKLIST

Content Quality

- [ ] **Specific and Detailed:** Story includes specific facts, names, numbers, and outcomes
- [ ] **Personally Focused:** Emphasizes YOUR actions and contributions, not just team efforts

- [ ] **Relevant to MSL Work:** Demonstrates skills and competencies relevant to MSL success
- [ ] **Authentic and Truthful:** Based on real experience you can discuss confidently
- [ ] **Appropriate Scope:** Significant enough to be meaningful but not overly complex

STAR Structure

- [ ] **Clear Situation:** Context is established without unnecessary detail
- [ ] **Defined Task:** Your role and objectives are clearly articulated
- [ ] **Detailed Actions:** Specific steps you took are described with enough detail
- [ ] **Measurable Results:** Outcomes are quantified where possible and lessons learned are identified

Delivery Preparation

- [ ] **2–3 Minute Length:** Story can be told completely in appropriate time frame
- [ ] **Natural Flow:** Transitions between STAR components feel conversational
- [ ] **Key Points Highlighted:** Most important elements are emphasized appropriately
- [ ] **Questions Anticipated:** Ready for follow-up questions about details or decisions
- [ ] **Multiple Applications:** Story can be adapted for different behavioral question types

---

PRACTICE AND PREPARATION STRATEGY

Step 1: Anecdote Inventory

Identify 8–10 professional experiences that demonstrate different competencies:

- Leadership/influence example
- Communication/presentation example
- Problem-solving example

- Relationship-building example
- Adaptability/resilience example
- Learning/development example
- Collaboration example
- Conflict resolution example

Step 2: Story Mapping

For each anecdote, identify which behavioral questions it could address:

Anecdote #1: ______________________________

____

Could address questions: ______________________________

____

Anecdote #2: ______________________________

____

Could address questions: ______________________________

____

Anecdote #3: ______________________________

____

Could address questions: ______________________________

____

Step 3: Delivery Practice

- Practice telling each story out loud multiple times
- Time yourself to ensure 2–3 minute delivery
- Record yourself to evaluate clarity and confidence
- Practice with friends or colleagues for feedback
- Prepare for common follow-up questions

Step 4: Adaptation Strategy

Practice adapting your stories to different question formats:

- Can you shorten the story to 90 seconds if needed?
- Can you extend with additional details if interviewer wants more?

- Can you shift emphasis to different aspects (leadership vs. technical skills)?
- Are you prepared to discuss what you'd do differently in hindsight?

SAMPLE STAR RESPONSE EXAMPLE

Question: "Tell me about a time when you had to present complex scientific information to an audience with varying levels of expertise."

STAR Response

Situation: "During my postdoc at Johns Hopkins, I was invited to present our latest research on cardiac biomarkers at a multidisciplinary grand rounds that included everyone from medical students to senior cardiologists, emergency medicine physicians, and hospital administrators."

Task: "My challenge was to present our complex findings about novel troponin assays in a way that would be meaningful to clinicians for patient care decisions, while also being accessible to learners and administrators who needed to understand the cost and implementation implications."

Action: "I restructured my typical research presentation into three layers. I started with the clinical problem everyone could relate to—the challenge of ruling out MI in the ED. Then I explained our research methodology using analogies rather than technical jargon. For the detailed results, I created decision trees showing how the new assay would change clinical workflows, and included cost-benefit analysis slides for the administrators. Throughout the presentation, I paused to check comprehension and encouraged questions from different audience segments."

Result: "The feedback was overwhelmingly positive—the emergency medicine director said it was the first biomarker talk that made him understand the practical implications, and two medical students approached me afterward to discuss research opportunities. Most importantly, the hospital implemented our recommended testing protocol within 6 months, which reduced average length of stay for chest pain patients by 4 hours. This experience taught me that effective scientific communication requires understanding your audience's different perspectives and motivations, then creating a narrative that addresses all of them—a skill I know will be essential for engaging with diverse healthcare providers as an MSL."

QUICK REFERENCE: BEHAVIORAL QUESTION CATEGORIES

CATEGORY	KEY FOCUS	WHAT THEY'RE ASSESSING
Leadership	Influence without authority	Strategic thinking, motivation skills
Communication	Adapting message to audience	Scientific communication, presentation skills
Relationships	Building trust and rapport	Stakeholder management, emotional intelligence
Problem-Solving	Creative solutions under constraints	Analytical thinking, resourcefulness
Adaptability	Handling change and setbacks	Resilience, learning agility
Learning	Acquiring new skills quickly	Growth mindset, intellectual curiosity
Collaboration	Working across differences	Teamwork, conflict resolution

Remember: The goal isn't to have perfect experiences, but to demonstrate how you think, learn, and grow through professional challenges—exactly the mindset needed for MSL success.

AI LEARNING GUIDE FOR MEDICAL AFFAIRS PROFESSIONALS: A STRUCTURED 12-MONTH PATHWAY FROM INTERVIEW PREPARATION TO CAREER LEADERSHIP

PHASE ONE: FOUNDATION BUILDING (MONTHS 1–2)

Goal: Interview readiness and basic competency
Time Investment: 2–3 hours/week

Learning Activities

- Complete "AI for Healthcare Professionals" course (Coursera)
- Create accounts: ChatGPT, Claude, Google Bard, OpenEvidence (free tiers)
- Practice basic prompts for literature summarization and email drafting
- Read *Harvard Business Review* articles on AI and industry publications

Week-by-Week Focus

Weeks 1–2: Conceptual understanding of AI types (ML, NLP, generative AI)
Weeks 3–4: Hands-on practice with 3 platforms, document 5 use cases
Weeks 5–8: Interview preparation and networking with AI-using professionals

Assessment Milestone: Can you confidently discuss three specific AI applications for MSLs, provide two personal examples, and explain key compliance considerations?

PHASE TWO: PRACTICAL APPLICATION (MONTHS 3–6)

Goal: Daily workflow integration and measurable productivity gains
Time Investment: 4–5 hours/week

Learning Activities

- Upgrade to premium AI platforms (ChatGPT Plus, Claude Pro)
- Explore specialized tools (Semantic Scholar, OpenEvidence, Elicit for research)
- Join LinkedIn AI groups and Reddit r/ChatGPT communities
- Maintain detailed prompt library and success metrics

Workflow Integration Schedule

Monday: Literature monitoring with AI assistance
Wednesday: Scientific content creation (narratives, summaries)
Friday: Competitive analysis and insight generation

Advanced Skills Development (Months 5–6)

- Multi-step prompt engineering for complex tasks
- AI-assisted presentation development
- Integration with CRM and project management tools
- Share learnings through internal presentations

Assessment Milestone: Demonstrate 40% reduction in routine task time, consistent AI content quality with proper fact-checking, and ability to teach others basic applications.

PHASE THREE: MASTERY AND LEADERSHIP (MONTHS 7–12)

Goal: Organizational thought leadership and strategic impact
Time Investment: 6 hours/week (Months 7–9), 4 hours/week maintenance (Months 10–12)

Strategic Activities

- Take executive AI courses and attend AI-focused conferences
- Develop AI implementation proposals for management
- Create training curricula for medical affairs teams
- Establish compliance frameworks and quality assurance systems

Leadership Development

- Present at medical affairs conferences on AI adoption
- Publish articles or blog posts on AI applications
- Lead organizational AI initiatives and vendor evaluations
- Mentor colleagues transitioning to AI-enhanced workflows

Advanced Tools and Resources

- Custom workflow automation platforms
- Enterprise AI solutions
- Industry expert network development
- AI vendor relationship building

Assessment Milestone: Evidence leadership in organizational AI strategy, measurable team impact, and recognition as internal/external thought leader in AI adoption.

SUCCESS METRICS AND CAREER IMPACT

Phase One Outcomes

- Interview confidence with specific AI examples
- Understanding of pharmaceutical AI compliance requirements
- Demonstrated learning agility and technology adoption

Phase Two Outcomes

- Documented productivity improvements and ROI
- Integration of AI into daily workflows without quality compromise
- Colleague training and knowledge sharing

Phase Three Outcomes

- Selection for AI-related projects and committees
- Performance review recognition for innovation
- External speaking opportunities and thought leadership
- Influence on technology adoption decision

IMPLEMENTATION GUIDELINES

Success Factors

- Consistent daily practice over intensive sessions
- Systematic documentation of learnings and best practices
- Focus on quality improvement alongside efficiency gains
- Balance experimentation with regulatory compliance

Critical Pitfalls to Avoid

- Over-reliance on AI without critical evaluation skills
- Neglecting compliance procedures and quality control
- Learning too many tools simultaneously
- Isolating AI learning instead of sharing knowledge

Continuous Learning Strategy

- Dedicate 1 hour weekly to staying current with AI developments
- Participate in healthcare AI professional communities
- Regularly reassess and optimize tools and workflows
- Maintain curiosity while developing healthy skepticism about AI capabilities

This structured approach transforms AI adoption from an overwhelming challenge into a manageable career development strategy that enhances both immediate performance and long-term professional trajectory in medical affairs.

Index

Note: Page numbers in *italic* refers to Figures.

For Product Safety Concerns and Information please contact our EU representative GPSR@taylorandfrancis.com Taylor & Francis Verlag GmbH, Kaufingerstraße 24, 80331 München, Germany